Foundations of Character

TEACHER EDITION

David Barton
and Nita Thomason

Tyndale House Publishers, Inc.
Carol Stream, Illinois

Visit Tyndale's exciting Web site at www.tyndale.com

TYNDALE and Tyndale's quill logo are registered trademarks of Tyndale House Publishers, Inc.

Video Produced by Coldwater Media
"Drive Thru History America" is a trademark of Coldwater Media, LLC.
Curriculum Produced by National Day of Prayer Task Force
and Tyndale House Publishers, Inc.
© MMVI National Day of Prayer Task Force

Drive Thru History America: Foundations of Character Teacher Edition
Drive Thru History America: Foundations of Character Homeschool Edition

Designed by Joseph Sapulich

Edited by Stephanie Voiland

Unless otherwise indicated, all Scripture quotations are taken from the *Holy Bible*, New International Version®, NIV®, Copyright © 1973, 1978, 1984 by International Bible Society. Used by permission of Zondervan. All rights reserved.

Scripture quotations marked KJV are taken from the *Holy Bible*, King James Version.

H1 Hummer® is a registered trademark of General Motors Corporation.

School Curriculum Kit: ISBN-13: 978-1-4143-1205-7   ISBN-10: 1-4143-1205-9
Homeschool Curriculum Kit: ISBN-13: 978-1-4143-1183-8   ISBN-10: 1-4143-1183-4
Teacher Edition: ISBN-13: 978-1-4143-1184-5   ISBN-10: 1-4143-1184-2

Printed in the United States of America

12 11 10 09 08 07 06
7 6 5 4 3 2 1

Contents

Introduction

As a teacher for this generation of students, you have a more challenging task than ever before. Your students need a solid foundation of content and skills in order to thrive in our rapidly changing culture. And somehow, beyond teaching the basics, you also want to instill in your students a strong sense of character. But how will you have the time—or the resources—to teach such lessons as good citizenship, leadership, and integrity?

Drive Thru History America: Foundations of Character is designed to address all these areas. This curriculum provides thorough historical content about the individuals and events surrounding the founding of the United States. The text, objectives, and activities are aligned with the National Council for the Social Studies standards. And integrated throughout the content, you will find values-based lessons and applications from the lives of our Founding Fathers and Mothers.

This curriculum will help young Americans understand the important contributions made by the men and women who led our nation during the Revolutionary era, as well as the character and faith of these individuals. Within these units, you will find a rich variety of primary sources that show the connection between the beliefs and actions of these individuals.

The men and women portrayed in this curriculum are worthy models for students today. As a result of studying the worldviews and actions of our Founders, students will obtain a more comprehensive understanding of the history of our nation and the world. When they apply these lessons to their own lives, they will be better prepared to live with integrity and to fulfill their responsibilities as American citizens. As students follow the examples of these men and women, they will come to realize, as their Founding Fathers and Mothers did, that they, too, can make a difference.

How to Use This Curriculum Guide

The curriculum is divided into nine units followed by a final assessment component—all of which are designed to meet state-mandated curriculum guidelines. The units include the following components:

Standards and Objectives

The teacher's guide lists the National Council for the Social Studies (NCSS) standards with which each unit aligns. The teacher's guide also includes student performance expectations for each unit. In the student edition, there are significant questions for students to preview at the beginning of the lesson and consider throughout the unit.

Fasten Your Seat Belt provides a brief introduction to the historical figure. Primary achievements of the Patriot are mentioned in this section. Also, significant questions for the student to consider will be previewed.

A Look in the Rearview Mirror focuses on a particular incident or series of events in the formative years of each character. Students will be encouraged to reflect on how these early lessons impacted the future of each individual.

Historical Marker gives students a glimpse into a significant contribution the Revolutionary figure made to the new nation. Stories included in this section provide the historical context for this individual and highlight his or her notable achievements. Students are encouraged to evaluate the contributions of the Founding Fathers as models of civic virtue.

School Zone Ahead offers teachers cross-curricular connections designed so that the content integrates various subject areas. Ideas for science, language arts, history, geography, math, technology, art, and family and consumer science activities are provided. Students identify various points of view and apply critical thinking skills as they interpret information, analyze data, and engage in various activities.

Right of Way highlights virtues exemplified in the lives of the historical figures. This segment allows students to glimpse character traits such as integrity and courage and to observe how these attributes defined their leadership styles and personal lives.

You're in the Driver's Seat places students in a position to examine their own lives—their thoughts and actions. Some of the exercises encourage independent reflection; others are designed to motivate students for action. Students are encouraged to apply critical thinking skills, draw conclusions, and make responsible decisions.

Worldview examines a significant question across various disciplines, such as philosophy, ethics, biology, sociology, and economics. This segment investigates the worldview that guided the men and women in this series. They understood that a foundation built on God's Word and moral character was the hope for the new nation. Students will examine the core beliefs that led to specific actions taken by these patriotic citizens.

Map Your Way includes actual words spoken by the Founders as they testified to their belief in the Creator. For those whose writings are scarce, eyewitness reports verify the authenticity of the Founders' relationship with God.

Drive Thru History is the video presentation for each character. Each DVD segment lasts approximately ten minutes. Discussion questions are included for guiding students into deeper understanding of the material presented.

Supplemental Teacher Material is found at the end of each unit. This is where you will find answer keys, as well as lists of topics you might select for further study with your students. These topics include geography/places, historical events/context, individuals and groups of people, and key terms. Additional resources for further reference are also listed for you or your students.

These influential Americans, who lived and served during the formative years of the United States, shared a legacy of faith and a commitment to both God and country. The goal of this curriculum is to restore their legacy and raise up a new generation of Americans who not only understand their heritage but who have the character to rebuild it, as they light the way for a brighter future.

Time Line

Benjamin Franklin
[1706-1790]

1732	publishes *Poor Richard's Almanack*
1746-52	conducts electricity experiments
1776	signs Declaration of Independence
1778	negotiates treaties with France
1787	attends Constitutional Convention

Benjamin Banneker
[1731-1806]

1737	becomes joint landowner
1753	builds wooden clock
1789	correctly predicts solar eclipse
1791	surveys land for Washington DC
1792	publishes his first almanac

George Washington
[1732-1799]

1753	goes on a diplomatic mission to the French
1754	begins serving as a colonel in the French and Indian War
1775	is named commander in chief of the Continental Army
1787	serves as president of the Constitutional Convention
1789	is elected first president of the United States

Haym Salomon
[1740-1785]

1772	moves from Poland to New York
1778	is sentenced by British to die for treason
1782	buys subscriptions in the National Bank
1781-84	loans over $200,000 to United States
1785	dies virtually penniless, holding $353,000 in almost worthless certificates of indebtedness and Continental currency

Abigail Adams
[1744-1818]

1764	marries John Adams
1775	sends letters reporting on the Revolutionary War
1776	lobbies against slavery and for women's rights
1784-85	reunites with John overseas while he works in foreign relations with England and France
1800	becomes the first woman to live in the White House in Washington DC

Benjamin Rush
[1745-1813]

1760	graduates from Princeton College
1768	receives medical degree
1776	signs Declaration of Independence
1777	serves as physician general of the Continental Army
1793	gives medical care during Philadelphia's yellow fever epidemic

Noah Webster
[1758-1843]

1777	leaves Yale to join the local militia
1778	begins teaching career
1783	publishes *The Blue-Back Speller*
1785	embarks on his book tour
1828	completes the first American dictionary

John Quincy Adams
[1767-1848]

1777	travels to France with his father
1825	becomes America's sixth president
1830	is elected to the House of Representatives
1841	defends Africans who seized the ship *Amistad*
1846	gets bill approved creating Smithsonian Institution

Lesson 1

NCSS Curriculum Standards

II. Time, Continuity, and Change

What happened in the past, and how am I connected to those in the past?

V. Individuals, Groups, and Institutions

What are the roles of institutions in society?

VI. Power, Authority, and Governance

How are governments created, structured, and changed? How can individual rights be protected within the context of majority rule?

X. Civic Ideals and Practices

How has the meaning of citizenship evolved?

Performance Expectations

Students will be able to:

1. Systematically employ processes of critical historical inquiry, such as using a variety of sources and checking their credibility, validating and weighing evidence for claims, and searching for causality.

2. Identify and describe examples of tensions between belief systems and government policies and laws.

3. Analyze and explain ideas and mechanisms to meet needs and wants of citizens, regulate territory, manage conflict, establish order and security, and balance competing conceptions of a just society.

4. Describe instances in which language, art, belief systems, and other cultural elements can facilitate understanding or cause misunderstanding.

5. Explain the origins and interpret the continuing influence of key ideals of the democratic republican form of government.

Lesson 1:
Faith and Freedom

Questions to Ask Yourself throughout This Unit

- On what foundations did the Founding Fathers base the new nation?

- How did the Founders understand the relationship between church and state?

- What worldview guided the Founders as they created a government for the new nation?

- Can freedom flourish without faith?

Did You Know . . . ?

- During a battle in the French and Indian War, four bullets pierced the coat of Colonel George Washington and two horses were shot under him, but he escaped without a wound.

- Haym Salomon, a Jewish immigrant from Poland, loaned his own money to support the Revolutionary cause, and Congress designated him "financier of the revolution."

- The first woman to live in the White House, Abigail Adams, was both a wife and mother of U.S. presidents.

- Thomas Jefferson, although not a mainstream Christian, considered Jesus the most important philosopher to have ever lived.

Fasten Your Seat Belt

On September 17, 1796, President George Washington delivered a speech known as his Farewell Address. In it, he emphasized two foundations, or "pillars," upon which this nation was built.

"I believe that religion is the only solid base of morals and that morals are the only possible support of free governments."
Gouverneur Morris, signer and penman of the Constitution

What were these foundations—these critical supports? The first and primary pillar was religion, and the second was morality, which Washington said was a product of the first. Virtually all of the Founding Fathers consistently declared that these two elements were vital for continued political success. In his Farewell Address, Washington said:

Of all the dispositions [viewpoints] and habits which lead to political prosperity, religion and morality are indispensable supports.

He went on to say that no one who tried to overthrow religion and morality could claim to be patriotic. He considered religion and morality to be "great pillars of human happiness . . . firmest props of the duties of men and citizens." We must flash back to the beginning, to the Pilgrims of Plymouth Plantation, in order to understand the key to the American experiment. The Pilgrims understood and first demonstrated that religion and morality were inseparable from civil society. They laid the original foundations for what has become the world's most successful civil government. They had a greater purpose—one that was beyond themselves. They believed they were part of a larger story.

A Look in the Rearview Mirror
The Pilgrims of Plymouth

In 1534, a new law made King Henry VIII the leader of the church in England; it also required all English people to be members of the Church of England (the Anglican church), over which Henry had just become the absolute authority. Many objected to being members of that Church or being expected to worship in a certain way; they believed that the Bible specified other ways of worship as well. Those who objected became known as "Dissenters." As punishment for refusing to worship the way he mandated, Henry burned the Dissenters at the stake or beheaded them. When Henry's daughter Elizabeth became queen, she took his position as head of the Church and continued his policy that all citizens attend Anglican services only. Those who disobeyed were fined, imprisoned, exiled, or executed.

There were two major groups of Dissenters. Some tried to purify the Church of England to remove the corruption and help it better align with the teachings of the Scriptures. This group became known as the Puritans. Others decided that it could not be purified—that the corruption was too deep and the persecution too severe. This group decided to withdraw from the Church, and they became known as Separatists (later called Pilgrims).

The Separatists honored God, studied the Bible, tried to live godly lives, and took their faith seriously. They wanted to worship freely and disapproved of the corruption that existed in the Church of England. Their homes were watched night and day by British authorities. Since remaining in England was dangerous, a group of Separatists moved to Holland, where they could enjoy greater religious freedom. They worked hard in Holland and made a decent living, but life in their newly adopted country proved difficult. The

Separatists wanted to maintain their English identity, and they regretted that their children were being raised as Dutch rather than English citizens.

Some American customs we can thank the Pilgrims for:
- *self-government*
- *the free enterprise system*
- *a workfare system (rather than a welfare system)*
- *the antislavery movement*
- *the practice of purchasing private property*

Therefore, in their continuing quest for religious freedom, they decided to move to America. In September 1620, after many difficulties, the forty-one Separatists joined with other travelers, including hired help and other "strangers," as they were called, to form a group of 102 men, women, and children who began the voyage to America aboard the *Mayflower*. When the group left Europe on their long voyage to America, Governor William Bradford named them Pilgrims. This title comes from Hebrews 11, KJV, in which a pilgrim is described as someone who is a temporary resident on earth, traveling through life on a journey to his or her real home in heaven.

Many difficulties challenged the sea travelers, including crowded conditions, sickness, and disagreements. The *Mayflower* averaged only two miles an hour on its journey to the New World. Furthermore, a terrible storm battered the ship for days, pouring waves of cold ocean water across the deck. As the storm raged, a deafening crack shook the *Mayflower*, and a main beam splintered. The passengers waited in terror for the storm to subside, but the turbulent waves continued to pound the vessel. After sixty-six days and nights at sea, they finally spotted land. However, they were not where they had expected to land; the storm and

fierce winds had blown the ship more than one hundred miles north of their intended location. Despite that shocking surprise, the Pilgrims believed that God had used the storm to direct them to Massachusetts instead of Virginia.

Before they went ashore they drafted a document (now called the Mayflower Compact) that formed a government by setting forth both the reason for their voyage and the process they would use in selecting their leaders. After the document was read aloud, the men (both Separatists and "strangers") signed it. Based on the teachings of the Bible (such as Exodus 18:21), the colonists chose their own governor and established self-government rather than the monarchal form they had experienced in Great Britain. They named their new colony Plymouth.

In the Compact, they also listed four reasons for coming to America: (1) to bring glory to God by spreading the Christian faith across America, (2) to plant a colony in the New World, (3) to form a united self-government, and (4) to make just laws that applied equally to everyone. The Mayflower Compact provided for government by mutual agreement—a revolutionary idea for that time period and a forerunner of what would later be captured in the Declaration of Independence, which calls for "the consent of the governed."

William Bradford, who would be elected governor more than thirty times, wrote a book about the Plymouth colony called *Of Plimoth Plantation*. He recorded that when the Pilgrims landed their ship in November of 1620, they "fell upon their knees and blessed [the] God of heaven, who had brought them over [the] vast and furious ocean."

The Pilgrims discovered that the land where they arrived was unoccupied. It had belonged to the Patuxet tribe, which had been destroyed four years earlier by an unknown illness. The Pilgrims found themselves in a land where they did not know how to live; they did not know how to hunt, fish, or farm in the New World, and they were unprepared for the ruthless and unforgiving climate. During their first three months in North America, nearly half of the colonists died.

How would those who were left be able to survive? God provided an answer for them through two Native Americans who befriended them and taught them how to live in the New World: Samoset and Squanto. These men also helped the Pilgrims make a peace treaty with the nearby Wampanoag tribe—a pact that lasted forty years.

1. Why did the Pilgrims come to America?

The primary reason the Pilgrims came to the New World was so that they could worship freely. In the Mayflower Compact, they wrote that they came to bring glory to God, build a new colony, form a united government, and create equal laws. Another reason was so that they could preserve their native culture and language within their families.

2. How did the plan of government outlined in the Mayflower Compact differ from the English government?

The government set up by the Mayflower Compact provided for government by the consent of the governed. In other words, those who lived in the new colony wrote the laws that governed their colony.

3. Describe the worldview (core beliefs) held by William Bradford and the Pilgrims of Plymouth.

William Bradford and the Pilgrims believed in God and followed the teachings of the Old and New Testaments of the Bible. They made decisions from a Christian worldview.

School Zone Ahead
Using Primary Sources (Research Activity)

A primary source is a firsthand or eyewitness account of an event. Letters, diaries, books, speeches, and journals written by people who participated in the event are considered primary sources. Other types of primary sources include paintings, photographs, and newspapers. These sources help historians and students gain an understanding, not only of events, but also of how people felt about and reacted to those events.

"Moral habits . . . cannot safely be trusted on any other foundation than religious principle nor any government be secure which is not supported by moral habits."
Daniel Webster, known as "Defender of the Constitution"

Primary sources from the colonial period, such as William Bradford's book *Of Plimoth Plantation*, are sometimes difficult to read because of language and spelling changes. For example, a letter that looks similar to an *f* is used in place of *s* in sixteenth- and seventeenth-century writing. This is because the alphabet at that time used two different symbols for *s*—one

symbol for a soft-sounding *s* and a different symbol for a hard-sounding *s*.

Secondary sources are derived from original documents. Sometimes modern historians change the meanings of the original texts when they write about historical events or delete certain sections of the text. This altering of history is called *revisionism*, and it means the deliberate alteration of historical facts to portray a new view of history. Compare the following statements from the Mayflower Compact. Does the modern version alter the original meaning of the document?

The Modern Version:

We whose names are under-written . . . do by these presents solemnly and mutually in the presence of God, and one of another, covenant and combine our selves together into a civil body politick, for our better ordering and preservation and furtherance of the

ends aforesaid. (Kenneth Davis, *Don't Know Much About History*, 1990)

The Original Version:

*We whose names are under-written **having undertaken, for the glory of God, and advancement of the Christian faith and honor of our king and country, a voyage to plant the first colonie in the northern parts of Virginia** do by these presents solemnly and mutually in the presence of God, and one of another, covenant and combine our selves together into a civil body politick, for our better ordering and preservation and furtherance of the ends aforesaid.*

Returning to primary sources helps us understand the original intent of historical documents. On the following pages, read each quotation and use the clues to figure out who said it. Then answer the corresponding questions.

WHO SAID IT?

"The only foundation for . . . a republic is to be laid in Religion. Without this there can be no virtue, and without virtue there can be no liberty, and liberty is the object and life of all republican governments."

Essays, Literary, Moral and Philosophical, 1798

Hints:
1. He has a medical college and countless hospitals across the country named after him.
2. He shares a first name with two other Founding Fathers.
3. This man's last name can also mean "to move forward with haste" or "to advance a football by running."

⚙ **What did this signer of the Declaration of Independence consider necessary for virtue?**

⚙ **What do you think is necessary for virtue today? Explain your answer.**

Quotation #1: Benjamin Rush. The Founders, including Benjamin Rush, expressed their belief that the American experiment was built on a foundation deeper than the law or even the Constitution. It was built on the Word of God as revealed in the Christian worldview and the Judeo-Christian ethic. In fact, the framers of our society acknowledged this as the basis of government in our founding document. Our forefathers considered every area of life sacred and saw no separation between the sacred and the secular; God's laws applied to all aspects of life.

WHO SAID IT?

"Without morals, a republic cannot subsist any length of time; they therefore who are decrying the Christian religion . . . are undermining the solid foundation of morals, the best security for the duration of free governments."

Letter to James McHenry, November 4, 1800

Hints:
1. This person was the last survivor of the signers of the Declaration. He died in 1832, at the age of ninety-six.
2. He shares a last name with the author of *Alice's Adventures in Wonderland.*
3. This man has a first name in common with the Prince of Wales, a former NBA basketball player (Barkley), and a cartoon character (Brown).

⚙ **What does this signer of the Declaration of Independence consider essential for a solid republic?**

⚙ **What do you think are the most important requirements for a successful government?**

Quotation #2: Charles Carroll. Success for the American form of government depended on moral people, firmly grounded in a Christian worldview. The Founders believed that the morals of the people were the only sure foundation for government and that morality was a product of adhering to the teachings of Scripture.

WHO SAID IT?

"The great pillars of all government and of social life [are] virtue, morality, and religion. This is the armor, . . . and this alone, that renders us invincible."

P A T R I C K

H E N R Y

Letter to Archibald Blair,
January 8, 1799

Hints:
1. This Patriot is famous for saying, "Give me liberty or give me death."
2. This man shares a first name with the patron saint of Ireland.
3. This man's last name is the same as that of eight former kings of England.

According to this Founding Father, what are the pillars of government and social life?

Do you think it's possible to have a government and society based on virtue, morality, and religion? Explain.

Quotation #3: Patrick Henry. The Founders understood that America's primary form of government had to be self-government. That is, if citizens did not govern themselves by the internal self-regulation provided through morality and religion, our form of political government would break down. Numerous others made similar pronouncements: America's self-government depended upon the individual self-government of citizens produced by morality through religion.

Historical Marker

The Puritans of the Massachusetts Bay Colony

The Pilgrims were not the only religious group that had difficulty with the Church of England. But while the Pilgrims decided to leave the Church, the Puritans wanted to stay and reform, or "purify," the Church. However, as a reward for their efforts, they became the victims of harsh persecutions, including having their noses slit or ears cut off, getting a brand on their foreheads, and being imprisoned. Consequently, many of the Puritans (almost twenty thousand) moved to the New World in search of religious freedom. Led by John Winthrop, they landed near the Pilgrims in 1630 but formed their own separate colony: the Massachusetts Bay Colony, where they established the city of Boston. They wanted to set an example by building a godly kingdom—what Winthrop had described as a "city on a hill" in his 1630 sermon "A Modell of Christian Charity." In that work, Winthrop reminded his fellow Puritans:

We are a company professing ourselves fellow-members of Christ . . . knit together by this bond of love. . . . We are entered into covenant with Him for this work. . . . For we must consider that we shall be as a city upon a hill, the eyes of all people are upon us; so that if we shall deal falsely with our God in this work we have undertaken and so cause Him to withdraw His present help from us, we shall be made a story and a byword through the world.

John Winthrop's phrase "city on a hill" comes from Matthew 5:14-16, in a section of the Bible called the Sermon on the Mount. Winthrop patterned his life on the teachings of the Bible. He and the other Puritan leaders (who served both as religious and governmental officials) crafted civil laws based on their interpretation of the Bible.

"The laws of nature and of nature's God . . . of course presupposes the existence of a God, the moral ruler of the universe, and a rule of right and wrong, of just and unjust, binding upon man, preceding all institutions of human society and of government."
John Quincy Adams

The Puritans emphasized not only the spiritual side of life but also the importance of an educated mind. As a result, they not only established the first successful college in America (Harvard) but also passed laws establishing a system of public education. Boston also became one of the most prosperous cities in the world at that time, and it became the center of publishing in America, producing schoolbooks and other books for children and adults. Yet despite the Puritans' enlightened attitudes in many areas, they enforced stiff and serious penalties for those who failed to obey the laws of the colony.

One example is the treatment religious individuals such as Roger Williams and Anne Hutchinson received for disagreeing with the Puritan leaders over the rights of conscience (or the right to hold beliefs that differed from the Puritan religion). The leaders of the Massachusetts Bay Colony brought them to trial and eventually banished them from the colony. Williams and Hutchinson went to other locations, helping establish new colonies with greater religious liberty. The right to worship freely was eventually established because of individuals such as Williams and Hutchinson, who willingly placed their lives in danger. They did this because they insisted on religious freedom—even from others of the Christian faith.

1. Compare and contrast the Pilgrims and the Puritans.

Both the Pilgrims and the Puritans adhered strictly to the Christian faith. However, the Pilgrims chose to separate from the Church of England, while the Puritans tried to maintain their relationship with the English Church, hoping to reform and purify the Church. People from both groups settled in the New World in a search for religious freedom.

2. Where did the phrase "city on a hill" originate, and what did John Winthrop mean when he used this phrase to describe the Massachusetts Bay Colony?

In Winthrop's sermon "A Modell of Christian Charity," he mentions the phrase "city on a hill," which comes from the Sermon on the Mount in Matthew 5:14. This is where Jesus called his followers to let their light shine and be a city on a hill that cannot be hidden. The group of Puritans led by John Winthrop hoped to purify the Church of England and establish a model Christian community in New England.

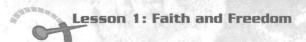
3. Why did Roger Williams and Anne Hutchinson leave the Massachusetts Bay Colony?

Although John Winthrop and the other Puritans came to America for religious freedom, they expected everyone in their colony to adhere to their beliefs as they believed God had commanded. Williams and Hutchinson were also Christians, but they did not agree with all the practices and beliefs of the Puritans in the Massachusetts Bay Colony. They thought every individual should be able to follow personal conscience, free of government defilement. The disagreements led to the Puritan leaders banning Williams and Hutchinson from their colony.

Stop and Ponder (for Group Discussion)

The Pilgrims and Puritans left their homes, suffered hardships, and sacrificed comfort in their quest for religious freedom. The First Amendment in the Bill of Rights to the U.S. Constitution guarantees American citizens freedom of religion. How do these protections impact your life?

The First Amendment of the Bill of Rights
"Congress shall make no law respecting an establishment of religion, or prohibiting the free exercise thereof; or abridging the freedom of speech, or of the press; or the right of the people peaceably to assemble, and to petition the government for a redress of grievances."

Right of Way: Faith

While the search for religious freedom brought English Pilgrims and Puritans to the New World, religious persecution in other European countries also brought people to America. For example, ancestors of John Jay, an author of the Federalist Papers and the first chief justice of the United States, fled France due to the persecution of the Huguenots (members of the Reformed Protestant Church of France) in the late seventeenth century. The primary motivation for European immigration to the New World during the seventeenth century was loyalty to faith and the desire to worship according to personal conscience. The influence of pastors during this search for religious freedom was significant. Clergymen fanned the flames of religious passion during the colonial period, and this pastoral

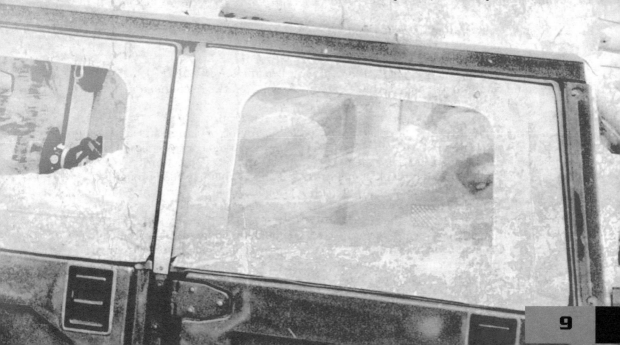

leadership linked the early colonists to the Revolutionary generation.

Christian ministers influenced thinking from Plymouth Rock to Independence Hall by preaching that fundamental law was the basis of all rights—in other words, natural and Christian rights were legal rights because they were a part of the law of God. The story of Revolutionary War–era pastor John Peter Gabriel Muhlenberg illustrates the link between faith and freedom in the minds of the early colonists and the Patriots.

"History will also afford frequent opportunities of showing the necessity of a public religion . . . and the excellency of the Christian religion above all others, ancient or modern."
Benjamin Franklin

On January 21, 1776, as armed conflict was breaking out across the colonies, Rev. Muhlenberg stepped to the pulpit wearing his pastoral robes. He read a biblical passage from Ecclesiastes 3: "There is a time for everything, and a season for every activity under heaven: a time to be born and a time to die . . . a time for war and a time for peace." As he closed his Bible, he stepped away from the pulpit and removed his robe, revealing the blue uniform of the American soldier. He called on the men of his congregation to stand with him and fight for the cause of liberty. Outside the church, the pastor ordered drummers to play as three hundred local men enlisted in the Eighth Virginia Regiment. Reverend Muhlenberg led these men and eventually earned the rank of major general in the Revolutionary army.

By the time the Founders wrote the defining documents of the new country, many issues regarding faith and freedom had been tested, but still the Founders struggled to define the relationship between church and state. Clearly the government they designed did not separate religion and politics. The influence of Christianity and the Bible was pivotal from the earliest flight of colonists from religious persecution to the refusal by the Revolutionary generation to submit to British oppression. Faith and freedom were central forces in colonizing and establishing the new republic.

Choose one of the following project options:

1. **Modern-Day Religious Persecution**
   Religious discrimination is not merely a problem of the past. Find out more about countries where people are persecuted for their faith, and then write a letter to an elected official alerting him or her of the human rights violations and religious persecution in one of these countries. You can find more information and addresses through one of these organizations:

   Voice of the Martyrs
   P.O. Box 443
   Bartlesville, OK 74005
   http://www.persecution.com

   International Christian Concern
   2020 Pennsylvania Ave.
   NW #941
   Washington DC 20006-1846
   http://www.persecution.org

2. **Mock Trial**
   Separation of church and state issues have sparked controversies in the United States for centuries. Choose an issue that has been brought to media attention in recent years, and create a mock trial to determine the constitutionality of a particular incident. Some possibilities include prayer in schools, the inclusion of evolution and/or intelligent design in the curriculum, the posting of the

Ten Commandments, the recitation of the Pledge of Allegiance in schools, and the display of nativity scenes at government buildings.

3. **Religious Persecution Map**
On a world map, identify various countries where groups were discriminated against during colonial times. (Some such countries include the Netherlands, Great Britain, Austria, France, Germany, and Brazil.) Shade in each country with a different color. Next to each country, write the name of the group or groups that were persecuted there (such as Jews, Quakers, Puritans, Mennonites, Huguenots, Pilgrims, Catholics, and Schwenkfelders). Do some research to determine where these groups settled in the New World, and draw an arrow (in the color that corresponds with each country) to that location.

4. **Statuary Hall Bio**
A statue of John Peter Gabriel Muhlenberg is located in the National Statuary Hall Collection of the United States Capitol. There are two citizens selected for the exhibit by each of the fifty states; Muhlenberg represents Pennsylvania. Using the Internet or an encyclopedia, choose one historical character honored in the Capitol collection and write a paragraph describing the person and why he or she was chosen. (See www.aoc.gov/cc/art/nsh/index.cfm.)

You're in the Driver's Seat
Exercising Faith

Filmmakers often present historical events, cultural phenomena, and factual information through documentaries. They prepare a storyboard before they begin filming.

1. **In a small group, choose a person from the list of colonial leaders your teacher provides. Research the historical figure and write down a list of important facts about each of the following topics:**

- **A formative incident from this person's youth or childhood**

- **His/her faith heritage**

- **Difficulties faced**

- **Sacrifices made**

- **Main contributions to society**

- **Lasting legacy**

2. **Make a storyboard by drawing pictures to illustrate four significant incidents in the life of your historical character. Be sure to include captions that describe what is happening in each frame.**

3. **Presentation: Share your storyboard with your class. If time allows, you might want to consider assigning parts and filming your documentary.**

William Bradford
- **He came to America with other Pilgrims in search of religious freedom.**

- **He helped draft the Pilgrims' plan of self-government, the Mayflower Compact, which created fair laws for the good of everyone.**

- **He played an important role in planting a colony; he trusted God as the Pilgrims tried to carry forth the vision they found in the Scriptures.**

- **He helped implement revolutionary but successful paradigms for the operation of state, church, businesses, social programs, and interracial relations.**

John Winthrop

- In his sermon "A Modell of Christian Charity," Winthrop defined the Puritan vision of establishing a colony as a city on a hill (see Matthew 5:14-16) to set an example for others to see and follow.

- Winthrop was the governor of the Massachusetts Bay Colony.

- He played a significant part in determining the role of religion in the colony's government.

Roger Williams

- Williams, a Puritan minister, disagreed with other Puritan leaders, believing that government should not punish citizens for their religious beliefs.

- He founded the second English colony to offer religious freedom in North America (Rhode Island—Maryland, founded two years earlier, had been the first) to persecuted Christians of all sects (including Puritans, Quakers, and Presbyterians—many of whom he stridently disagreed with) and also to Jews.

- He advocated religious tolerance and freedom of worship and also maintained excellent relations with the Native Americans.

Anne Hutchinson

- Hutchinson believed and taught others that a good conscience toward God and faith alone were enough to be considered a good Christian.

- She claimed to receive revelations directly from God. She held meetings in her home in which she taught both men and women her interpretation of the Scriptures, which advocated a covenant of grace rather than of works.

- Because she refused to abide by some of the Puritan laws, she was expelled from the Massachusetts Bay Colony and went first to Rhode Island and then to New York.

Thomas Hooker

- Clergyman Thomas Hooker and his Puritan followers, after being persecuted for their faith in England, founded the colony of Connecticut in their search for greater religious and political freedom.

- He penned the first written constitution in the New World, the "Fundamental Orders of Connecticut" (considered a direct predecessor of the U.S. Constitution), and he allowed non-Puritans and nonlandowners to vote.

- He is known as the "father of American democracy."

William Penn

- Penn, a Quaker, wanted to build a colony based on Quaker beliefs but open to people of all faiths.

- Penn was influential in establishing good relations between colonists and Native Americans.

- Penn was one of the first Americans to argue for the rights of women.

- Penn also established the city of Philadelphia—a Greek word meaning "city of brotherly love." Pennsylvania attracted people of all faiths and races from around the world and became one of America's largest colonies; it became the first "melting pot" in America.

Clearly, faith not only played a critical role in the lives of many significant colonial leaders but also was foundational to the governments they designed. As the early colonies drafted their civil laws, most declared that the Bible was the basis of their laws and thus their foundation for right and wrong. The ultimate source of American law was the revelation of God as found in his creation and his Word. The Christian worldview played a critical role in the lives of the colonial leaders and in the establishment of the great American political system.

"The people of this . . . country, profess the general doctrines of Christianity, as the rule of their faith and practice. . . . We are a Christian people, and the morality of the country is deeply engrafted upon Christianity, and not upon the doctrines or worship of those impostors [other religions]."
U.S. Supreme Court, 1892

Worldview
History: What Can I Learn from the Past?

God directs the course of history through the lives of individual men and women. The story of America explodes with meaning when we realize that God used people—the Pilgrims, the Puritans, the Founders, and millions of ordinary citizens—to achieve his purposes for humanity. The biblical worldview on which this nation is founded led Americans to see that no separation existed between the sacred and the secular. Every area of life was sacred and was to be lived "as working for the Lord" (Colossians 3:23). The key to the American experiment was the people's deep conviction that underneath their individual lives was a deeper purpose. They were part of a larger story—a story well beyond their own little stories, well beyond their own place in history.

Map Your Way
"I always consider the settlement of America with reverence and wonder, as the opening of a grand scene and design in Providence [God], for . . . mankind all over the earth."
John Adams, in a diary entry, 1765

It is obvious that faith played a critical role in the formation of governmental systems during the colonization of America. In the following lessons, we will see that it was the Founding Fathers and Mothers of the eighteenth century who considered the relationship between faith and freedom foundational for the great experiment they designed. An important question for Americans today is whether freedom can survive without faith. As you begin this study of the Founders of this nation, think about these questions:

- **What is the relationship between faith and freedom?**

- **Can a free society succeed without people of faith?**

- **What role should religion play in government?**

- **How can a religiously diverse nation balance respect for all backgrounds with its moral foundation?**

"Religion and good morals are the only solid foundations of public liberty and happiness."
Samuel Adams, signer of the Declaration of Independence

DVD Reflection

Watch the DVD segment for Lesson 1 and complete the following activities:

Drive Through History America
Foundations of Character

Dave Stotts describes eight American citizens who helped build this nation. Which person sounds most intriguing to you?

Benjamin Franklin

Haym Salomon

Dr. Benjamin Rush

Abigail Adams

George Washington

Noah Webster

Benjamin Banneker

John Quincy Adams

Up until now, what has been your opinion on learning about history?

What is one freedom you are glad for in this country?

For Further Study

Geography

Mount Vernon
Plymouth Plantation
Holland
Massachusetts Bay Colony
Boston, Massachusetts
Plymouth Rock
Independence Hall
Lexington, Massachusetts
Concord, Massachusetts

Historical Context

Church of England
Mayflower
Mayflower Compact
Declaration of Independence
Of Plimoth Plantation
"A Modell of Christian Charity"
Sermon on the Mount
The Federalist Papers

Significant Individuals and Groups

Alexis de Tocqueville
Pilgrims
King Henry VIII
Dissenters
Queen Elizabeth I
Puritans
Separatists
Governor William Bradford
Patuxet tribe
Samoset
Squanto
Wampanoag
Gouverneur Morris
John Winthrop
Roger Williams
Anne Hutchinson
John Jay
Huguenots
John Peter Gabriel Muhlenberg
Patrick Henry

Terms

pilgrim
self-government
monarchy
free enterprise
workfare
welfare
revisionism
chief justice
secular
Providence

Additional Resources

John Winthrop, *The Journal of John Winthrop, 1630–1649* (Cambridge, Mass.: Belknap Press, 1996). Winthrop's personal journal tells his perspective of the founding years of the Massachusetts Bay Colony.

Francis J. Bremer, *John Winthrop: America's Forgotten Founding Father* (New York: Oxford University Press, 2003). This biography of John Winthrop traces his spiritual struggles and contributions to the founding of the colonies. It includes his disagreements with Roger Williams and Anne Hutchinson.

William Bradford, *Of Plymouth Plantation 1620–1647* (New York: Random House, 1981). This modern language reprint of William Bradford's personal journal highlights the founding years of the Plymouth colony.

Os Guinness, *The Great Experiment: Faith and Freedom in America* (Colorado Springs: NavPress, 2001). This book offers readings and commentary on the Founders' framework for establishing the American experiment. It explores the role of faith in a free society, in terms of both the constitutional leaders and our society today.

David Noebel and Chuck Edwards, *Thinking Like a Christian* (Nashville: Broadman & Holman, 2002). This teaching textbook explains the Christian worldview in relation to various disciplines.

Lesson 2

NCSS Curriculum Standards

I. Culture

How do belief systems, such as religion or political ideals, influence culture?

V. Individuals, Groups, and Institutions

What are the roles of institutions in society, how am I influenced by institutions, and what is my role in institutional change?

VIII. Science, Technology, and Society

How can we manage technology so that the greatest number of people benefit from it?

II. Time, Continuity, and Change

What happened in the past, and how am I connected to those in the past?

Performance Expectations

Students will be able to:

1. Identify the values and virtues of Benjamin Franklin, and describe ways his beliefs and attitudes helped shape our country.

2. Apply knowledge of how groups and institutions, such as those designed by Benjamin Franklin, worked to meet individual needs and promote the common good.

3. Identify historical examples of the interaction and interdependence of science, technology, and society, and seek reasonable and ethical solutions to problems that arise when scientific advancements and social norms or values come into conflict.

4. Identify and apply lessons from Franklin's life to their own experiences.

Lesson 2:
Benjamin Franklin

Questions to Ask Yourself throughout This Unit

- How did the values and virtues of Benjamin Franklin shape the new American nation?

- How did Franklin's organizational abilities and interactions with others promote the common good?

- How did Benjamin Franklin's scientific experiments transform society?

- What twenty-first century lessons can this eighteenth-century man teach?

Fasten Your Seat Belt

"My grandfather is not like other old people." This is what Benjamin Franklin's grandson Benny Bache wrote in his journal about one of America's most beloved Founding Fathers. It's no wonder—when Benjamin Franklin was almost eighty years old (at a time when the average life span in the colonies was only thirty-five years), he swam across the broad and deep Seine River near Paris—just to teach his grandson Benny how to swim!

Benjamin Franklin was a man of diverse talents. He was a scientist, business strategist, diplomat, writer, printer, humorist, inventor, governor, and statesman. Yet despite his notable achievements, Franklin considered himself just an ordinary individual; he trusted the common people and was comfortable with the idea that everyday citizens made America strong. Much of this attitude can be attributed to his religious upbringing as a Quaker, for Quakers did not place a strong emphasis on external differences or class distinctions. Rather, they emphasized the equality of all people and the ability of each individual to hear from God and then do what was right.

Franklin's fingerprints can be found on many of the most important government documents of America's early years: the Albany Plan of Union (1754), the Declaration of Independence (1776), the treaty of alliance with France (1778), the peace treaty with England (1783), and the U.S. Constitution (1787). Through his writings and his life, he exalted middle-class virtues and was known in America and across the world as "the first American."

He initially worked tirelessly to help Britain resolve her differences with the American colonies and avoid the American Revolution. But when those early efforts failed, Franklin threw himself wholeheartedly into the Revolution. He not only served the cause with distinction as a statesman in America and in Europe but also, as a member of the Constitutional Convention, helped build the governmental foundations that have caused our country to be a world leader for more than two centuries. The United States—unlike so many other nations—has not had a national revolution every few decades; on the contrary, we are now the longest ongoing constitutional republic in the history of the world, having thrived for more than two centuries under the Constitution that Benjamin Franklin helped write.

A Look in the Rearview Mirror
Water, Wind, and Fire: The Elements of Invention

The group of boys tramped across the marsh to a favorite swimming hole near Boston Bay. Their leader, Benjamin Franklin, splashed into the water, eager to show the others his new invention. By pulling large, flipperlike sandals onto his feet and by fastening oval paddles to

his hands, Ben glided through the water with increased speed. His friends were impressed, as usual. Ben was always experimenting with new devices.

His ingenious ideas sometimes led to trouble, however—such as the day when the boys took stones that were intended for the construction of someone else's house. He said in his autobiography, "In the evening when the workmen were gone home, I assembled a number of my playfellows and we worked diligently, like so many emmets [busy ants], sometimes two or three to a stone, until we brought them all to make our little wharf." Franklin told the story of this shameful theft not because he was proud of his actions but in order to illustrate his father's lesson that "nothing was useful which was not honest." Franklin quickly learned this lesson and put aside dishonest ways.

Ben's early interest in water and in kites remained with him throughout his life and led to future endeavors of great usefulness to the entire world. One of those famous endeavors began when he was an adult and watched a performance that "surpris'd and pleased" him. A traveling scientific showman rubbed a glass tube to create static electricity. Then he moved the tube close to the feet of a boy who was hanging from the ceiling by silk cords. This caused large sparks to shoot between the tube and the boy's feet. The sparks were caused by electricity, but no one at that time knew much about electricity or understood how it operated.

The show fascinated Franklin, and he and his friends started experimenting with the unknown phenomenon of electricity too. Ben realized that electricity acted like a fluid, and he thought up words associated with the brand-new concept of electricity that we still use more than two and a half centuries later—words such as *positive* and *negative*, *charges*, *battery*, *condense*, and *conductor*. He also discovered what he called "the wonderful effects of points," which inspired him to invent the lightning rod to protect houses and barns from bolts of lightning. This invention prevented the lightning fires that previously had destroyed so many structures.

Ben's most famous discovery involving electricity was performed with an audience of only one other person: his twenty-one-year-old son, William. Turbulent clouds were gathering over Philadelphia in June 1752, when Benjamin and William hoisted a silk kite into the sky during a lightning storm. Benjamin had attached a sharp-tipped metal wire to the top of the kite and tied a key to the bottom of the kite string. The kite was flying high; the lightning was flashing around it. When Ben noticed the filaments of the kite string begin to bristle, he extended his knuckle toward the key at the end of the string, and an electric spark jolted his body. Electricity had traveled from the lightning, into the metal wire at the top of the kite, and down along the kite string, and had then shocked him when he touched the metal key tied to the string. Other scientists had previously hypothesized a relationship between lightning and "electrick fire" [electricity], but Franklin was the first to design an experiment to prove the connection. His experiment showed that electricity was a force of nature and—like gravity—could have enormous benefits if it could be tamed and made practical. Franklin's scientific experiments with electricity made him famous in America and a celebrated hero across Europe.

Franklin emphasized the usefulness of science, and his many inventions were designed for practical uses—to benefit mankind. For example:

- In order to be able to see his dinner plate right in front of him as well as the person sitting across the table, he invented bifocal eyeglasses to help correct his poor eyesight so he could see both near and far.

- To maximize heat from fireplaces (heat often escaped up the chimneys in homes built in the 1700s) and to minimize the smoke created by fireplaces, he invented the wood-burning stove (called the Franklin stove).

- When he worked as postmaster of the colonies, he invented an odometer to count the revolutions of wagon wheels so that he could calculate the shortest and most efficient routes for all wagons to travel.

- He poured a teaspoon of oil into a pond and observed that it not only spread for half an acre but also that oil smoothed the surface ripples in water; he invented a "magic cane" that emitted droplets of oil to still turbulent water.

- In order to extend working hours for farmers, he invented daylight saving time, which called for setting clocks ahead an hour in the summer to allow an additional hour of daylight in the evening.

He explored medical issues, such as the cause of colds and the effects of lead poisoning.

He made calculations about the Gulf Stream that were useful to navigators.

He designed an organlike musical instrument called an armonica. Its pleasant sounds were the result of various amounts of water filling several small glass containers.

As a young child, Franklin had been taught the principle in Romans 14:7 that "none of us lives to himself alone," so Franklin sought to benefit all humankind in the scientific realm just as he did in the political realm. In his scientific endeavors, Franklin did not request patents for his inventions but instead developed strong international friendships and encouraged an atmosphere of scientific cooperation. His celebrity status as an inventive scientist actually gave him a political platform and made him a credible spokesman before many governments, where he advocated for the rights of average citizens. Franklin not only helped the common people by freeing them from monarchs and giving them republican self-government, but he also helped them by his many inventions. Turgot, a famous Frenchman, described Franklin's impact on both science and government: "He snatched lightning from the sky and the scepter from tyrants."

1. The idea that Franklin had "snatched lightning from the sky" prompted debate among the French. They wondered whether the lightning rod was a victory of man over nature or of man over God. In our modern world, scientific developments sometimes surpass ethical understanding. What recent scientific accomplishments challenge ethical positions?
Cloning, therapeutic cloning, chimeras (part animal, part human), in vitro fertilization, and embryonic stem-cell research are a few examples of scientific technologies medically available but ethically questionable.

2. Explain how Franklin's religious views affected his decisions.
Franklin's Quaker heritage caused him to see all individuals as equal before God and influenced him to share his inventions with everyone. Thus, he forfeited considerable personal profit.

3. In a spirit of cooperation, Franklin shared his discoveries with other scientists. How does this compare with scientific investigations today? What does his refusal to obtain patents for his Philadelphia fireplace and his electrical inventions say about his character?
Many inventors acquire patents so they can preserve sole ownership and can control who uses the inventions as well as profit financially from their innovations. His refusal to obtain patents shows he cared more about helping others than about making money.

4. List advantages of cooperation in the arenas of sports, government, education, and the workplace.
In many cases, cooperation shortens the time needed to achieve excellence and also leads to higher levels of service and profitability.

5. The maxim "If you build a better mousetrap, the world will beat a path to your door" leads to the conclusion that competition

promotes excellence. Give three examples of how competition can lead to improvement.

Competition has led to the development of better products in the automobile industry, telecommunications, technology, pharmaceuticals, space exploration, the service sector, tourism and travel, entertainment, and many other enterprises. Sports achievements and academic endeavors also increase due to the competitive spirit.

Stop and Ponder (for Group Discussion)

What position do you hold on various scientific and ethical issues, such as physician-assisted suicide, stem-cell research, partial-birth abortion, and cloning?

What standards do you use to make those decisions?

Historical Marker
A Time to Work

Franklin was not only a statesman and a celebrated scientist known for his inventions, but he was also a famous printer characterized by homespun humor and middle-class values. This was significant in a society that often emphasized a kind of social snobbery. Franklin was an outspoken advocate of our nation being led by "the middling people," as he called them, not rich elitists. Probably the most famous of all of his printing works was *Poor Richard's Almanack*. This almanac was the most popular one ever in American history.

Almanacs were small pamphlets that contained calendars, typical weather information (such as the average amount of rain per month and the usual time of the first frost or snowfall), and astronomical information (including the time of sunrise and sunset on each day, the schedule of solar or lunar eclipses, and the cycles of the moon from new to full). This information was especially useful for farmers to decide when to plant and when to harvest, as well as for business owners to know when to open and close their shops. (Many of the guidelines for business owners were outlined in "blue laws"—rules that dictated citizens' conduct and morals.) Additionally, almanacs usually had a number of interesting short stories and often contained wise proverbs and sayings.

Franklin published his almanac under the pen name Richard Saunders. Hence, it was "Poor Richard's" rather than "Poor Ben's" almanac. One of the characteristics of Franklin's almanac was its use of humor to deliver wise truths. Here are two of "Poor Richard's" witty statements:

⚙ **Three may keep a secret if two of them are dead.**

⚙ **He's a fool that makes his doctor his heir.**

Although many eulogies and speeches of praise were delivered about Franklin, he himself had written the eulogy that he wanted inscribed on his tombstone:

The Body of Benjamin Franklin, Printer,
(Like the cover of an old book,
Its contents torn out,
And stripped of its lettering and gilding,)
Lies here, food for worms.
But the work shall not be lost,
For it will, as he believed, appear once more,
In a new and more elegant edition,
Revised and corrected
By the Author

Benjamin's career as a printer spanned several decades, and he became one of the most famous printers not only in this country but also in the world. In fact, when word of Franklin's death reached Paris, the National Assembly of France declared three days of mourning, and French printers organized a printing ceremony to show their respect for the noted American printer. As one printer read a eulogy for Franklin, the other printers set the speech into type and only moments later delivered a freshly printed copy of the eulogy.

Franklin was a hero celebrated across the world at his death; and even though many nations grieved his passing, the displays of admiration and honor would have astonished the young Benjamin Franklin who first straggled into Philadelphia as a novice printer.

In telling the story of how he became a printer, Franklin described himself as "the youngest son of the youngest son for five generations back." His father arranged for him to learn a trade by placing him as an apprentice under an older brother who was involved in the printing business. Franklin clicked instantly with the printing business and even worked diligently to improve his own writing style. Under the pseudonym Silence Do-good, he submitted satirical essays attacking the Boston pro-monarchal aristocratic establishment.

However, the bright and innovative teenager often clashed with his older brother, and following a series of disagreements, seventeen-year-old Ben left his brother and headed to Philadelphia. Arriving in the city, the dirty, hungry traveler sauntered up Second Street almost completely penniless, with only "a Dutch dollar and a copper shilling" in his pocket, as he says in his autobiography. He bought three puffy rolls and "having no room in my pockets, walk'd off with a roll under each arm, and eating the other." He passed by the home of a prestigious family (the Reads) and was seen by his future wife, Deborah, who thought he made "a most awkward, ridiculous appearance." It was a Sunday, so he joined many "clean-dressed people" and sat down in a Quaker meetinghouse.

After trying to get himself established in Philadelphia through forays into several business ventures, the young printer eventually managed to establish his own printing business. With the help of his wife, Deborah, Franklin achieved considerable success, which he attributed to "industry and frugality." As a young printer, he followed Poor Richard's maxim "Early to bed and early to rise, makes a man healthy, wealthy, and wise." Following a strict regimen, he got up before sunrise and worked long hours. Often he was seen pushing his own cart of paper through the Philadelphia streets. (He knew that his own industrious habits would make a favorable impression on those who watched.) Franklin worked hard in an effort to achieve an early retirement from business, which freed him to spend

his time in activities he considered to be of greater worth. His diligence was rewarded with remarkable success, and in his early forties he retired (although he kept his printing business) and pursued other interests—science, politics, and diplomacy. However, regardless of his successes in so many other arenas, he always considered himself a printer, signing his name "Benjamin Franklin, printer."

During his years as a printer, Franklin acquired a valuable communication skill that would aid him in his endeavors the rest of his life: He learned how to engage in conversations without directly contradicting others and how to present his own opinions with an attitude of modesty. He honed his communication skills and ideas through a network of friends he had organized. That group discussed a wide range of topics and strove to improve themselves and their community. As Franklin wisely noted, "The good [that] men may do separately is small compared with what they may do collectively."

Detour: The Junto
Franklin's group of working-class peers was known as the Junto—a word that means "joined." This group of civic-minded friends met together for discussions and planning every Friday. They created the first public library in America and started the first volunteer fire department, night-watchmen corps, and insurance program.

Another one of Franklin's early endeavors to serve his fellow Americans was the establishment of the Philadelphia Hospital to care for those in need. Franklin chose an interesting logo for the hospital seal—it was a picture of the biblical Good Samaritan caring for the injured stranger and placing him on his donkey; around the seal were words from Luke 10:35 (KJV): "Take Care of Him and I Will Repay Thee."

Create your own junto by breaking into small groups. Answer the following questions, which were used by Franklin and his friends:

1. What new story have you lately heard agreeable for telling in conversation to benefit others? (Have you heard a story lately that would be helpful for all of us to hear?)
2. Do you know of any fellow citizen who has lately done a worthy action deserving praise and imitation? Or who has committed an error proper for us to be warned against and avoid? (Has anyone in our community done something that would be good for us to do too? Has anyone in our community done something that we should try to avoid?)
3. Have you lately observed (or seen in the media) any encroachments on the just liberties of the people? (Have you seen or heard about something [in the media or live] that took away someone's rights or freedom?)

School Zone Ahead
Maxims (Language Arts Activity)

Benjamin Franklin's maxims appeared throughout his writings. His maxims are like bite-size pieces of wisdom. Consider the following sayings, and write short definitions of their meaning. Then analyze whether you agree with the maxim and how you could apply its message in your life.

Choose one of the following activities about Franklin's maxims:

1. **Translate Maxims**
   Write ten of the maxims in modern-day language. Analyze whether you agree with each and how you could apply its message to your life.
2. **Narrate a Maxim**
   Choose one of these maxims and write a fictional parable to illustrate the lesson the maxim teaches.
3. **Act Out a Maxim**
   Create a mime or a script for a skit that communicates the message of one of Franklin's maxims. Then perform the skit for the rest of your class or another audience.
4. **Draw a Maxim**
   Create a poster or a comic strip that depicts someone experiencing the truth contained in one of these proverbs.

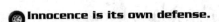

Innocence is its own defense.

He does not possess wealth; it possesses him.

Eat to please thyself, but dress to please others.

Do good to thy friend to keep him, to thy enemy to gain him.

Deny self for self's sake.

The rotten apple spoils his companions.

He that can have patience can have what he will.

The worst wheel of the cart makes the most noise.

As we must account for every idle word, so we must for every idle silence.

An empty bag cannot stand upright.

When the well's dry, we know the worth of water.

Little strokes fell great oaks.

Necessity never made a good bargain.

Work as if you were to live a hundred years; pray as if you were to die tomorrow.

To err is human, to repent divine; to persist devilish.

Well done is better than well said.

Who is rich? He that rejoices in his portion.

The first female editor in America was Benjamin Franklin's sister-in-law, Ann Franklin. She became editor of the Newport Mercury *when her son died, and she continued her work there until her death in 1763.*

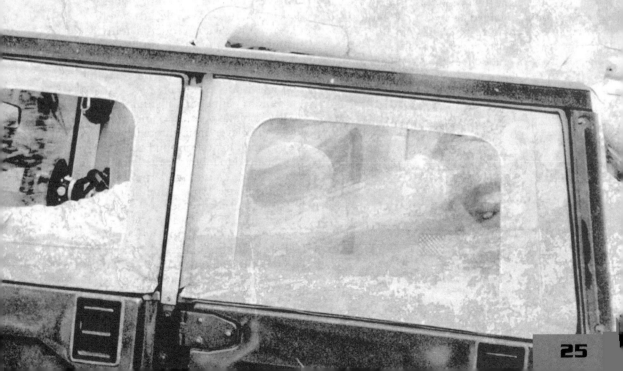

Right of Way: Commitment
A Time to Laugh, a Time to Pray

Dr. Benjamin Franklin (now an adult and a statesman for America) stood for nearly an hour in front of Alexander Wedderburn, the solicitor general of the British Privy Council, who raked the American diplomat over coals hotter than a Franklin stove. It was January 29, 1774, nine days after news of the Boston Tea Party had hit the London papers. (Years before that event, Franklin had been sent to Europe by the Continental Congress to advocate for the rights of the American colonists.) Wearing his old-fashioned full-bottomed wig and a suit of blue velvet, Dr. Franklin stood silently in the amphitheater of Whitehall (the British government) as the furious Wedderburn leveled angry, inflammatory, and irrational charges against the American diplomat. The British solicitor general accused Franklin of being the "prime conductor" of the troubles in Massachusetts, even though Franklin had not been in America at the time! The British Privy Council blamed all their problems in the colonies on Franklin, who stood silently and did not show a trace of emotion, even as the hostile crowd jeered and laughed at him.

JOIN, or DIE.

The crowd may have laughed at Franklin, but the actions of the British in 1774 had been no laughing matter for the colonists. Yet through all their difficulties, there could have been no better representative in England for the Americans than Ben Franklin.

Franklin had frequently proven his ability to assist the American colonists in the most adverse circumstances. In 1753 during the French and Indian War (when it was the colonists and the British fighting the French and the Native Americans), Franklin had been sent on his first diplomatic mission to the Native American chiefs of the powerful Six Nations along the American frontier. Then he organized a volunteer militia to protect Pennsylvania from French and Native American attacks. When British general Braddock needed supplies for his army, which was protecting Pennsylvanians from the French and Native Americans, Franklin used his personal influence to gather 150 wagons with four horses each, an additional 259 packhorses, and an assortment of food and supplies to aid in General Braddock's quest. And in 1765—a decade before his encounter with Wedderburn in Britain—Franklin successfully argued in the British parliament on behalf of the Americans against the hated Stamp Act, which was eventually repealed.

Franklin penned many humorous essays to make political points, and his jokes and clever antics brought him many social invitations and connections that he used to lobby for the Patriot cause. In fact, after Wedderburn's scalding attack against him, Franklin wrote several more pieces using satire and sarcasm, but he was unable to achieve an understanding with the British. Franklin realized that the time had come to go home to Philadelphia.

The Second Continental Congress was already gathering in Philadelphia when Franklin arrived in 1775. The day after he returned, he was selected as a delegate to Congress—the oldest of its sixty-three members. Although a few suspicious members believed Franklin was secretly a British loyalist, most did not, and Congress therefore appointed him to serve on a select committee of five distinguished members to write a document announcing America's independence from England. The document they wrote was the Declaration of Independence.

The Continental Congress approved the separation from Great Britain on July 2, 1776, and then voted to approve the Declaration on July 4, knowing that those votes might cost them their lives because King George would surely send troops against them once he saw the Declaration. When the document was officially signed a month later, on August 2, the Congress's president, John Hancock, said, "There must be no pulling different ways. We must all hang together." To which Franklin replied, "Yes, we must, indeed, all hang together—or most assuredly we shall all hang separately!"

When America embarked on its quest for independence, the leaders of the new nation realized that in order to defeat the British, they would need assistance from other nations. To secure the help of the French, Congress dispatched Benjamin Franklin to France for a dangerous, complex, and secret mission.

Paris welcomed the famous American, and he used his celebrity status to the advantage of the colonies. Wearing his soft fur cap and bifocal glasses, Franklin, it's been said, created an image of purity and other virtues promoted in the New World. Using both his humor and his adept diplomatic skills, Franklin engaged in a campaign to win the hearts and minds of the French. As a result, the United States and France signed two treaties: a treaty of commerce and a treaty of military alliance. On the evening of the treaty signing, Franklin wore his old blue velvet suit. When asked why he had chosen to wear that suit, Franklin replied, "To give it a little revenge: I wore this coat on the day Wedderburn abused me at Whitehall." Now he had worn it on the day the French became the colonists' allies against the British. Franklin's ability to use humor and be flexible enhanced his effectiveness as a diplomat and Patriot for more than thirty-five years.

By the time Benjamin Franklin was in his eighties, many considered him to be the greatest philosopher of the age. The American Revolution was over and America had established its own government, but citizens feared that the government they had created during the American Revolution under the Articles of Confederation was in crisis and that the stability of the new republic was in danger. The Articles of Confederation had proved too weak; America was still too divided. It needed something stronger and better—something more unifying. A gathering of fifty-five of the nation's leading statesmen (including Franklin) was therefore called to propose a solution. That gathering was called the Constitutional convention, and it eventually produced the U.S. Constitution.

The wise old sage was driven by a desire for stability and unity during that convention. He willingly compromised several of his own ideas and proposals (such as a single legislature rather than a plural legislature, a multiple executive rather than a single executive, and nonpayment of government officials) in order to bring unity to the gathering. There were many debates—often heated; many of the delegates and states held strong and often opposing opinions, and the discussions grew rancorous. After listening to the controversies, the eighty-one-year-old Franklin offered his advice in a stirring speech and suggested that the delegates begin sessions each morning with prayer.

Here is part of his speech, addressed to George Washington, president of the Constitutional Convention:

Mr. President:

I have lived, sir, a long time, and the longer I live, the more convincing proofs I see of this truth—that God governs in the affairs of men. . . . I firmly believe this; and I also believe that without His concurring aid we shall succeed in this political building no better than the builders of Babel [Genesis 11:6-9]. . . . I therefore beg leave to move that henceforth prayers imploring the assistance of Heaven, and its blessings on our deliberations be held in this Assembly every morning.

Extended Excerpt from Franklin's Speech to the Constitutional Convention
Mr. President:

The small progress we have made after four or five weeks close attendance and continual reasonings with each other . . . is, methinks, a

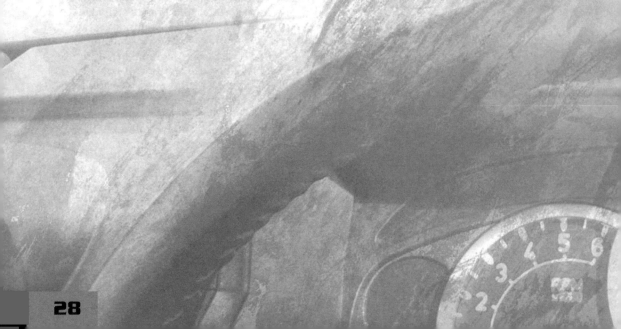

melancholy proof of the imperfection of the human understanding. . . . In this situation of this Assembly, groping as it were in the dark to find political truth, and scarce able to distinguish it when presented to us, how has it happened, sir, that we have not hitherto once thought of humbly applying to the Father of lights to illuminate our understanding? In the beginning of the contest with Great Britain, when we were sensible of danger, we had daily prayer in this room for the Divine protection. Our prayers, sir, were heard, and they were graciously answered. All of us who were engaged in the struggle must have observed frequent instances of a superintending Providence in our favor. . . . And have we now forgotten that powerful Friend? Or do we imagine we no longer need His assistance? I have lived, sir, a long time, and the longer I live, the more convincing proofs I see of this truth—that God governs in the affairs of men. And if a sparrow cannot fall to the ground without His notice [Matthew 10:29], is it probable that an empire can rise without His aid? We have been assured, sir, in the Sacred Writings, that "except the Lord build the house, they labour in vain that build it" [Psalm 127:1]. I firmly believe this; and I also believe that without His concurring aid we shall succeed in this political building no better than the builders of Babel [Genesis 11:6-9]. . . . I therefore beg leave to move that henceforth prayers imploring the assistance of Heaven, and its blessings on our deliberations, be held in this Assembly every morning before we proceed to business, and that one or more of the clergy of this city be requested to officiate in that service.

His speech seemed to change the tone of the convention. A three-day recess was called, during which time many of the delegates attended church together. When they returned to the convention, delegates commented on the new positive attitude among the group; tempers had calmed, and instead of the convention breaking apart, it held together.

Franklin's desire that reliance on God be a part of official governmental actions became reality. For more than two centuries since Franklin's speech, the U.S. Congress has opened each day's work in the House and the Senate with— as Franklin described it—"prayers imploring the assistance of Heaven, and its blessings on our deliberations."

Many people today are surprised to learn that Benjamin Franklin offered such religious recommendations, for some describe him as one of the least religious Founding Fathers. Yet religious faith was very important to Ben Franklin. In fact, when Thomas Paine was in the process of preparing his *Age of Reason* attacking religion and urging a secular society, it was Benjamin Franklin who rebuked Paine for his secular ideas. Franklin warned: *The consequence of printing this piece will be a great deal of odium [hate] drawn upon yourself, mischief to you, and no benefit to others. He that spits into the wind, spits in his own face. . . . Think how great a portion of mankind . . . have need of the motives of religion to restrain them from vice, to support their virtue. . . . I would advise you, therefore, not to attempt unchaining the tiger, but to burn this piece before it is seen by any other person. . . . If men are so wicked with religion, what would they be if without it?*

Franklin strongly objected to a secular society that would exclude religion from public life. He not only drafted a statewide prayer proclamation for his own state of Pennsylvania, but he also recommended Christianity in the state's public schools and worked to raise church attendance in Pennsylvania as well. Benjamin Franklin was a supporter of many American ideals: science and invention, liberty and individual freedom, and the role of religion in daily life.

1. **Explain the double meaning of the pun Wedderburn used when he described Franklin as "prime conductor."**
   Franklin was the first to use the word "conductor" to describe a body capable of transmitting electricity. Wedderburn accused Franklin of being the prime conductor—that is, the principal transmitting body—of the difficulties between Great Britain and America.

2. **Many of the signers of the Declaration of Independence suffered great losses as a result of their efforts for the new nation. Find out what happened to these men and their families. (Some possibilities include the following signers: Carter Braxton, John Hart, Francis Lewis, Arthur Middleton, Edward Rutledge, and Richard Stockton.)**
   Answers will vary.

3. **What were Benjamin Franklin's views on the role of religious faith? Give at least two examples to substantiate your answer.**
   Benjamin Franklin's faith affected the way that he viewed all others around him, causing him to be an advocate for the common people. His faith caused him to recognize

that people need God's help, and he therefore called for prayer during the Constitutional Convention. His faith affected the way he viewed life after death, evidenced in his epitaph that refers to life after death and meeting the Author of life.

Stop and Ponder (for Group Discussion)

Tell about a person you know who has made a sacrifice for something or someone important to him or her.

How much would you be willing to sacrifice to preserve liberty for your country?

Detour

Those fifty-six signers of the Declaration of Independence did "hang together"—and it cost them greatly. In the Declaration, they announced that they were "appealing to the Supreme Judge of the world," and then they pledged their "lives, fortune, and sacred honor" to achieve American independence. Nine of those who signed that document did not live to see independence become a reality. Another dozen lost their homes, estates, and every material belonging when their property and possessions were deliberately destroyed by the British. Three lost their children to British bullets. Several of those who signed were tortured as prisoners of war—as were several of their wives. It was costly for them to protect freedom for our sakes (as it has been for many Americans since then), but they were willing to make those sacrifices so that we could enjoy the liberties we now possess.

You're in the Driver's Seat
Gaining Insight

Benjamin Franklin wrote the story of his life in his now-famous *Autobiography*—he wanted other people to learn from his lessons and experiences. He examined his life, and near the end of it he wrote, "I would rather have it said, 'He lived usefully,' than, 'He died rich.'" Franklin also sought to strive for "moral perfection" by acquiring thirteen virtues.

Franklin's Thirteen Moral Virtues

Temperance	*Industry*	*Tranquility*
Silence	*Sincerity*	*Chastity*
Order	*Justice*	*Humility*
Resolution	*Moderation*	
Frugality	*Cleanliness*	

Examining one's life gives insights for growth. Answer the questions on the following four topics as you think about your own life.

1. **Heroes**
   Name people who have influenced you positively. What attributes caused you to admire or respect them? How are you different because of them?
2. **Hard Times**
   What difficulties have you faced? How did these challenges shape you as a person? What did you learn from the hard times?
3. **Highlights**
   What do you consider the best times of your life? Why? How can you use these good times to strengthen yourself and others?
4. **Hopes**
   What are your hopes for the future? List career, family, citizenship, and community goals.

Choose one of the following projects to help you think more about what your own autobiography might include.

1. **Collage Autobiography**
   Divide a piece of twelve-by-eighteen-inch manila paper into four parts, titling each section with one of the

above topics. Make a collage from magazine pictures and printed words or phrases to illustrate each section of your autobiography.

2. Virtues Autobiography
Look over Benjamin Franklin's list of thirteen virtues. If you had to choose thirteen attributes that *you* would consider the most important for "moral perfection," what would they be? On a calendar or daily planner, assign one virtue each day for the next thirteen days. Each day, try to focus your actions and thoughts on that particular trait, and keep a journal of your progress (both successes and failures). At the end of the thirteen days, write a reflection on the experiment, thinking about these questions: What did you learn about yourself from this project? Do you think moral perfection is possible? Is it something we should strive for? Explain your answers.

3. Talk-Show Autobiography
Create a talk-show script, imagining a talk-show host interviewing two guests for today's show: you and Benjamin Franklin. Come up with questions for the host to ask based on the four questions on page 28, and decide how each of you would answer the questions. You can act out the talk show in front of a live audience or record the production on camera.

Worldview

Philosophy: What's Real, and How Do I Know What's True?

Many people attempt to discover how the world works through philosophy. They try to answer such questions as, Who am I? Why am I here? Where am I going? Benjamin Franklin's scientific experiments indicated his understanding of who he was and why he was here; his epitaph indicates his understanding of where he thought he was going after he died.

Contrary to the popular view of his day that women should be trained only in household matters and the arts, Benjamin Franklin supported education for women. He worked with a woman in Holland who ran a printing press after her husband's death, and this led him to recommend "education for our young females, as likely to be of more use to them and their children, in case of widowhood, than either music or dancing, by preserving them from losses by imposition of crafty men, and enabling them to continue, perhaps, a profitable [business]."

Map Your Way

"Here is my Creed. I believe in one God, the Creator of the Universe. That He governs it by His Providence. That He ought to be worshipped."
Benjamin Franklin

When Franklin touched the key during his kite experiment, an electric spark jolted his body and he learned a truth about electricity. Similarly, when he considered the key concept of his life philosophy, he turned to God in order to know what was true. Consider these questions:

Why are you here?

Where are you going?

Benjamin Franklin used at least nine pseudonyms (pen names) when writing newspaper articles or letters to the editor. Six of these were women's names, and he used one of them in particular—Polly Baker—to examine the negative way women were treated in the eyes of the law.

DVD Reflection

Watch the DVD segment for Lesson 2 and complete the following activities:

Benjamin Franklin
The First American

Dave Stotts says that Ben Franklin's inventions were designed for usefulness and to benefit people.

Three benefits you enjoy as a result of Franklin's ingenuity and creativity:

1.

2.

3.

Franklin understood the value of working cooperatively. He said, "The good men do separately is small compared with what they may do collectively."

Two positive results from Franklin's work with others:

1.

2.

If Ben Franklin thumbed a ride in your Hummer,
where would you take him?

For Further Study

Geography
Seine River (Paris)
Boston Bay
Gulf Stream
Philadelphia, Pennsylvania

Historical Context
Albany Plan of Union
Declaration of Independence
Republican self-government
Blue laws
British Privy Council
Boston Tea Party
Whitehall
Six Nations
British Parliament
Stamp Act
Second Continental Congress
Single vs. plural legislative government
Multiple vs. single executive government

Significant Individuals and Groups
Quakers
Alexander Wedderburn
General Edward Braddock
King George III
John Hancock
Thomas Paine
Ann Franklin

Terms
lightning rod
bifocal eyeglasses
Franklin stove
odometer
daylight saving time
armonica
patent
eulogy
solicitor general
satire
philosophy

Additional Resources

Walter Isaacson, *Benjamin Franklin: An American Life* (New York: Simon & Schuster, 2003). This best-selling biography shows how Benjamin Franklin helped define his own time and ours. Using his homespun humor, democratic values, and philosophical pragmatism, he served the Revolutionary cause with distinction.

Benson J. Lossing, *Lives of the Signers of the Declaration of Independence* (Aledo, Tex.: WallBuilder Press, 1995). This book, originally published in 1848 by eminent nineteenth-century historian Benson J. Lossing, provides a brief biography of each signer of the Declaration.

Harry Clinton Green and Mary Wolcott Green, *Wives of the Signers: The Women behind the Declaration of Independence* (Aledo, Tex.: WallBuilder Press, 1997). This book describes the women who, alongside their husbands, experienced the trials and triumphs of the struggle for independence and the challenge of building a new nation.

Tim Baker, *The Way I See It* (Carol Stream, Ill.: Tyndale House, 2005). This is essentially a worldview book for teens (loosely inspired by Chuck Colson's book *How Now Shall We Live?*). It delves into the questions listed under Map Your Way: "Why are you here?" and "Where are you going?"

http://www.ushistory.org/franklin. This site includes Franklin's autobiography, a time line, quotations, and information about the Junto.

Os Guinness, *Time for Truth: Living Free in a World of Lies, Hype, and Spin* (Grand Rapids, Mich.: Baker Books, 2002). This book articulates and defends a worldview based on absolute truth in an age of relativism.

Lesson 3

NCSS Curriculum Standards

I. Culture

How do belief systems, such as religion or political ideals, influence culture?

IV. Individual Development and Identity

Why do people behave as they do, and how do individuals develop from youth to adulthood?

V. Individuals, Groups, and Institutions

What are the roles of institutions in society, how am I influenced by institutions, and what is my role in institutional change?

X. Civic Ideals and Practices

How has the meaning of citizenship evolved, and what is the balance between rights and responsibilities?

Performance Expectations

Students will be able to:

1. Compare and contrast the way different groups meet human needs and concerns.

2. Describe the ways religion, gender, ethnicity, and socioeconomic status contribute to the development of a sense of self.

3. Describe the role of institutions in furthering both continuity and change.

4. Examine the origins and continuing influence of key ideals of the democratic republican form of government, such as individual human dignity, liberty, justice, and equality.

LESSON 3:
Dr. Benjamin Rush

Questions to Ask Yourself throughout This Unit

- What principles and beliefs shaped Dr. Benjamin Rush? What do we learn about his character and motives from the way he approached medicine and interacted with people?

- What attributes helped Benjamin Rush stand firm under difficult circumstances?

- What foundational institutions are needed for a healthy society?

- How do you respond when you see an underdog? What do you do when you see something unjust? Are your actions consistent with what you believe?

Fasten Your Seat Belt

What do you do when you see something that's unfair? When you see a bully mistreating someone weaker, do you watch and then walk away? Or do you try to intervene and help? One of the signers of the Declaration of Independence, Dr. Benjamin Rush of Philadelphia, dedicated his life to standing up for those in need, as well as for those who were treated unfairly.

Dr. Rush thought the British oppression of the American colonies was unjust, so he stood up against Great Britain. He believed the bondage of African-Americans was wrong, so he fought slavery. He realized schooling for women was lacking, so he pioneered educational opportunities for them. He observed that the conditions for prisoners were often unreasonable, so he promoted prison reform. He recognized that treatment for the mentally ill was not only insufficient but often inhumane, so he demanded change. He saw that medical treatment and hospitals for wounded soldiers were inadequate, so he advocated improvement. He knew medicine for the poor was unavailable, so he provided treatment. This was the mantra of his life—seeing needs and finding solutions. Not only was Dr. Rush active in so many different areas, but understanding that the pen is mightier than the sword, he also wrote widely on those subjects.

Dr. Rush's advocacy for social justice had a profound impact on the new nation. As a reformer, he changed the face of the culture and helped the downtrodden; as an educator, he improved the quality of education and made it more available for all; as a physician, he benefited humanity through his discoveries; and as a statesman, he touched the lives of all Americans and secured freedom for millions. In fact, when he died in 1813, he was heralded by newspapers, Founding Fathers, and other leaders of the day as one of the nation's three most notable individuals, ranking along with George Washington and Benjamin Franklin.

A Look in the Rearview Mirror
Father of American Medicine

In the summer of 1793, a yellow fever epidemic struck Philadelphia. At that time, no one knew what caused yellow fever, and during the next one hundred days, one-tenth of the population in Philadelphia died. Understandably, fear descended on the city. Families boarded up their houses and retreated to the country, until the roads heading out of Philadelphia were jammed with panic-stricken citizens. The city became like a ghost town; only the creaking wheels of funeral hearses carrying the dead to unmarked graves interrupted the silence.

Nearly all the physicians fled the city along with the citizens, but Dr. Benjamin Rush was not among them; he refused to leave. He even urged his own medical apprentices to stay with him and help the sick. He believed that God had called him to medical service, and he told his students, "I may fall a victim to the epidemic, and so may you, gentlemen. But I prefer, since I am placed here by Divine Providence, to fall in performing my duty." Dr. Rush and many of his students therefore stayed in the city and attacked the plague, helping sick citizens. But their brave commitment eventually proved costly to many of them.

Rush believed that female education was of utmost importance, because "the first impressions upon the minds of children are generally derived from women."

With the eastern sky still black as the ink on his quill pen, Dr. Benjamin Rush dragged his weary body out of bed, lit a candle, and read the messages on scraps of paper that had been pushed under his door during the night. He saddled his horse and headed up Walnut Street to treat the first of seven patients he examined before 5:00 a.m. At every stop it was the same: The sick complained of sore throats, violent fevers, and abdominal burning. Often their skin had a yellow tinge, and sometimes a long black streak marred the middle of their tongues. The dreaded diagnosis remained consistent: yellow fever. Rich families tried to buy his services, offering extravagant sums of money to obtain preferential treatment, but Dr. Rush refused to be bought by the rich. Instead, following the teachings of his Christian faith, he treated the poor and the rich just the same. During the height of the epidemic, Dr. Rush treated as many as one hundred patients each day, and time constraints required that he turn away another fifty or sixty daily.

As the plague persisted, the doctor shortage intensified. During one period, only three physicians remained in Philadelphia, trying to care for six thousand ill individuals. Rush himself contracted the fever at least twice, sometimes treating patients from his own sickbed. At least three of his medical apprentices died during the epidemic. As Dr. Rush recorded in his notes, "My ingenious pupil, Mr. Washington, fell a victim. . . . Mr. Stall sickened in my house. . . . Scarcely had I recovered from the shock of the death of this amiable youth, when I was called to weep for a third pupil, Mr. Alston, who died . . . the next day." Since no one knew what caused the illness, Dr. Rush experimented with many treatments as he tried to save lives. Some of his methods, such as bloodletting, caused controversy, but he tried everything he could in his persistent fight against the deadly disease. He reported that by the last weeks of the epidemic, nineteen of twenty patients who followed his prescribed treatment plan survived.

Benjamin Rush had first faced the reality of death at the young age of six, when his own father died. Following that tragedy, Benjamin went to live and study with his uncle, the renowned scholar Rev. Dr. Samuel Finley. The lessons he learned from his clergyman uncle in those early years influenced him the remainder of his life. Rush graduated from Princeton College at the age of fourteen and decided to pursue a career in medicine. He served six years in the colonies as a medical apprentice, then continued his studies in Scotland.

In searching to make medical treatments more effective, Dr. Rush investigated many unexplored areas, even using his own digestive system in heroic experiments. He and his friend William Penny once ate a meal of beef, peas, bread, and beer; they then took a dose of alkali. After enough time for the food to digest, Benjamin and William gulped down a dose of tartar emetic, which caused vomiting. Up came their dinner. They tested the contents for acid. They duplicated the experiment, substituting veal for beef and water for beer. The third time, they repeated the experiment by eating chicken and cabbage. They concluded that gastric digestion is a chemical process similar to fermentation. This was an important new scientific and medical discovery with far-reaching implications.

When Benjamin Rush returned to Philadelphia in 1769, he was one of the best-trained physicians in America. But he had returned at a time when the American Revolution was beginning to brew and tensions were rapidly escalating between Great Britain and the colonies. Rush set up a medical practice, and it flourished. Because he was a Christian, he believed that it was his duty to help others, just as he would later do during the yellow fever epidemic. He not only treated the rich, who could pay for his services, but he also treated the poor, who couldn't. In fact, his medical records show that on one day, he treated sixteen patients but charged only one of them. Rush taught at three medical schools simultaneously, and some of his new medical treatments and discoveries—as well as his support for the Patriot cause—produced controversy; but he did not let the sharp criticisms deter him.

In 1776 America separated from Great Britain, and the Revolution officially began. The next year the Continental Army sought physicians for the battlefield. They enlisted Dr. Rush and placed him as one of the chief physicians overseeing medical treatment for the wounded. The young doctor had opportunities to apply his knowledge, and his sharp understanding produced lasting and positive results (for example, Dr. Rush discovered a method for curing lockjaw—an often fatal malady in his day). Although Rush worked diligently and faithfully in the military hospitals, the lack of supplies and the poor conditions exasperated him. He criticized his superiors, suggested improvements, and demanded reform, but he was stonewalled. He knew that so much more good could be done, but the inadequacy of the organizational and bureaucratic structure frustrated him to the point that he resigned in protest. But he continued to help in other ways, because quitting was not part of his nature—as was later proved by his refusal to run away from the yellow fever epidemic of 1793.

Dr. Rush practiced medicine for about half a century and eventually became one of the most famous doctors in American history. He even earned the title "father of American medicine." He was known not only in America but also around the world, and many leaders from other countries consulted him for medical advice and assistance. He received numerous awards from foreign kings and leaders, and on his death, condolences were sent from rulers across the globe. During his life, Dr. Rush personally trained three thousand medical students, whose impact spread throughout the country and even the world.

1. **In 1777, conditions in the Continental Army so frustrated Benjamin Rush that he resigned in disgust. But when the yellow fever epidemic plagued Philadelphia in 1793, the forty-seven-year-old Dr. Rush willingly sacrificed his own safety to provide the best possible care for the sick and dying. What do you think caused Benjamin Rush to respond as he did in each situation?**

Dr. Rush was always committed, first and foremost, to serving his patients and providing them with the most effective medical care. While an army surgeon, he was handicapped by the rules and decisions of his superiors (which often differed from his), thus preventing him from administering effective medical treatments. Since Dr. Rush was a famous physician, his resignation focused attention on the many problems in the army's medical treatments, thereby allowing them to be addressed. During the yellow fever epidemic, he personally made the decisions regarding patients, so he was able to provide the best and most effective treatments. He quit with the purpose of improving a situation, not because his circumstances were too difficult.

2. **Dr. Rush encouraged his apprentices to stay and treat the sick during the yellow fever epidemic. What happened to them as a result? If you had been one**

of the apprentices, what would you have done, and why?

At least three of Rush's apprentices died during the epidemic.

3. What does Dr. Rush's refusal to accept bribes for his medical treatment say about his character and motives as a physician?

Helping the sick, not earning money, was the motivation for Dr. Rush's work. Therefore, he would not allow money to dissuade him from his calling. He was a man of Christian conviction, and he believed that the rich and the poor should be treated equally.

Historical Marker
An American Dream

The year was 1809. Dr. Benjamin Rush awoke with a start; his dream was still reverberating through his mind. In his dream, he had pictured a history book of the United States, and the page he saw referred to his old friend John Adams. The book recorded an extraordinary event: the renewal of the friendship between John Adams and Thomas Jefferson. Rush dreamed that a rich correspondence grew from the renewed friendship of the two and that both men died at nearly the same time.

Dr. Rush wondered about his dream, for at the time, John Adams and Thomas Jefferson were mortal enemies and did not write or talk to each other. In fact, the dispute between the two had been going on for almost a decade. The icy relationship between Rush's fellow Founding Fathers troubled the wise old physician; he pondered a way to be a middleman for reconciliation, for his Christian faith taught him that he was not only to be a peacemaker (see Matthew 5:9) but also that he was to bring about reconciliation whenever possible (see 2 Corinthians 5:18). Dr. Rush finally wrote his old friend John Adams about the dream. As Rush signed his name to the letter, he recalled signing another document—a remarkable document both Adams and Jefferson had worked on—the Declaration of Independence.

Benjamin Rush had first recognized the growing rift between Great Britain and the colonies while studying medicine overseas in Scotland. Upon his return to America, he began writing essays on American independence but

41

was harshly criticized. Many claimed that a doctor should not be involved in such issues. However, Dr. Rush persisted—and he recruited others who shared his views. He encouraged Thomas Paine (who had recently emigrated from England) to write a series of articles that would help prepare the minds of American citizens to separate from Great Britain. Rush suggested the title *Common Sense* for the articles, and Paine's pamphlet was an immediate best seller; it sold half a million copies at a time when America had scarcely 4 million inhabitants. Paine's pamphlet uncapped a volcano of support for American liberty and turned the tide of public opinion toward independence. Rush's efforts led to friendships with other like-minded Patriots, such as John Adams and Thomas Jefferson, and his own state of Pennsylvania sent Dr. Rush as a delegate to the Continental Congress.

In Congress, Jefferson and Adams worked feverishly on the document declaring liberty from the mother country; and eventually the fifty-six members of Congress—including Dr. Rush—signed the document: the Declaration of Independence. Having worked with Adams and Jefferson, Rush knew that both were indispensable to American liberty. In fact, historian David McCullough calls Jefferson the "pen" of the Declaration of Independence and Adams its "voice." After the Revolution, their ideas shaped the new republic. Rush, a close friend of both men, regularly corresponded with the two, calling Adams and Jefferson the "North and South Poles of the American Revolution"—that is, they formed the central axis around which the American world revolved.

Rush worked with Abigail Adams (John Adams's wife) to establish the Young Ladies Academy of Philadelphia, one of America's first educational institutions for women.

When John Adams became president, Jefferson became his vice president, but a rift was growing between the two men. Each headed a political party that opposed the other; Adams headed the Federalists and Jefferson the Anti-Federalists. Conflict between the two parties became so fierce that it eventually prompted a duel between two of the party leaders—Aaron Burr the Anti-Federalist and Alexander Hamilton the Federalist. Hamilton died in the fight. When Jefferson defeated Adams in the 1800 presidential election, their relationship had become so icy that

Adams left the capital the night before Thomas Jefferson's inauguration.

It was Benjamin Rush's dream and letter that started the thaw between the two ex-presidents. Rush encouraged Adams to write to Jefferson and mend their differences. Adams listened to Rush and took the first step by writing to Jefferson. Eventually a correspondence started between the two, and the ice in their relationship melted. In fact, over the next twenty-four months, Adams and Jefferson wrote fifty letters to each other—after a decade of complete silence! Those letters between the two gave Americans in later generations a better understanding of the Revolutionary War period and insights into the establishment of the new nation.

Interestingly, just as Dr. Rush had seen in his dream fifteen years earlier, Jefferson and Adams died on the same day: July 4, 1826—exactly fifty years to the day both had signed the Declaration of Independence. The peacemaking role of Dr. Rush—and Adams's and Jefferson's willingness to forgive one another—demonstrates the character of all three Founding Fathers.

Choose one of the following activities related to Benjamin Rush's life:

1. More Than a Dream
A dream prompted Dr. Benjamin Rush to intervene in the conflict between Jefferson and Adams. Look at the list below and select one individual whose dreams influenced history. Create a comic strip or write a play script that depicts the dream and the events surrounding it.

- **Scientists/Inventors:** Friedrich August Kekulé von Stradonitz, Elias Howe, and Niels Bohr all claim that a dream assisted in their scientific discoveries.

- **Historical Figures:** Emperor Constantine and Harriet Tubman both saw visions that influenced the course of their lives.

- **Biblical Figures:** Joseph (Genesis 37; 40), Daniel (Daniel 2; 4), and Pilate's wife (Matthew 27) all had or interpreted dreams that impacted history in some way.

- **Musicians:** Beethoven, Paul McCartney, and Billy Joel say some creative inspiration came from a dream.

2. Peace by the Pen
Benjamin Rush's correspondence with Thomas Jefferson and John Adams was instrumental in the reconciliation between these two men. Imagine you are Rush, and write a letter to each of them. Describe your dream about their reconciliation, the positive qualities of the other individual, and the reasons they should try to restore their friendship.

3. Metaphorical Monikers
Dr. Rush used the metaphor "North and South Poles" to describe John Adams and Thomas Jefferson, and modern historian David McCullough calls Adams and Jefferson the voice and the pen of the Declaration of

Independence. Using these images as a starting point, create a collage or a poster depicting the role these two men played in U.S. history. Include a paragraph about each of them, explaining how the visual aspects of your project apply to them.

School Zone Ahead
Candidates' Forum (Social Studies Activity)

Adams and Jefferson held different views on the role of the federal government, and political parties sprang up to represent those holding each viewpoint. The Federalists (Adams's supporters) wanted a strong, active federal government; Jefferson's party (the Anti-Federalists) favored a weaker, less active federal government. Federalists considered the checks and balances system an essential safeguard against corruption; Jefferson's party gave less priority to the military, opposed taxes, and resisted growth of the federal government.

Two major political Parties dominate American politics today, as well: the Republican and Democratic Parties. The role of the federal government continues to divide Americans. Many believe a bigger, stronger federal government better protects people and solves problems, while others prefer limited power for the federal government, believing problems are solved better at the state and local levels and through the private sector.

Each election year civic organizations, churches, schools, and other groups sponsor candidate forums so that voters can better understand the policy positions of those running for office. (Also, politically neutral Web sites, such as www.vote-smart.org, offer candidates' positions to voters.)

Your teacher will divide the class into five groups.

Group 1: John Adams
Research John Adams's position on each of the following issues:

- **the role of the federal government**
- **states' rights**
- **slavery**
- **the United States' role in the French Revolution**
- **the creation of the U.S. Navy**

Assign group members to fill the following roles: researchers, recorder, and someone to portray John Adams in the forum.

Group 2: Thomas Jefferson
Research Thomas Jefferson's position on the following issues:

- **the role of the federal government**
- **states' rights**
- **slavery**

● the United States' role in the French Revolution

● the creation of the U.S. Navy

Assign group members to fill the following roles: researchers, recorder, and someone to portray Thomas Jefferson in the forum.

Group 3: Democratic Party
Research the position of the Democratic Party on the following issues:

● federal budget

● the economy and jobs

● health care

● immigration

● abortion

● crime

● traditional marriage

● foreign policy

Assign group members to fill the following roles: researchers, recorder, and people to portray Democratic candidates in the forum.

Group 4: Republican Party
Research the position of the Republican party on the following issues:

● federal budget

● the economy and jobs

● health care

● immigration

● abortion

● crime

● traditional marriage

● foreign policy

Assign group members to fill the following roles: researchers, recorder, and people to portray Republican candidates in the forum.

Group 5: Forum Moderators
Research and set the format for the two candidates' forums (one forum between Jefferson and Adams, and one between Democrats and Republicans). The group will decide on questions for the candidates. They will also determine time allotments for opening statements, responses to questions,

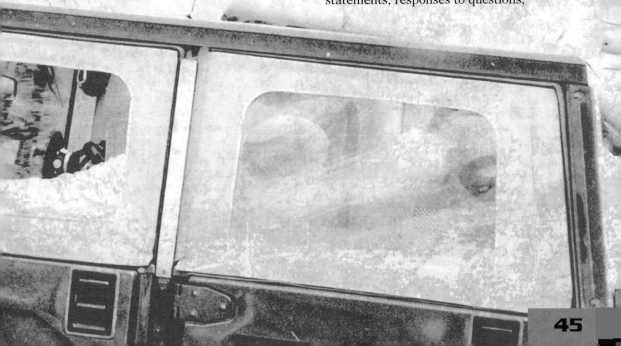

rebuttals, and closing statements. Students will be chosen to serve as forum moderator and timekeeper.

Right of Way: Compassion

Benjamin Rush showed compassion by promoting peace and agitating for reform. These traits may seem contradictory, but genuine compassion requires various responses. As a compassionate peacemaker, Rush resolved conflict, settled disagreements, and stopped fights. As a compassionate reformer, he campaigned for change, championed causes, and promoted social justice. Truly, he believed and lived the words he had signed his name to in the Declaration of Independence: that "all men are created equal and are endowed by their Creator with certain inalienable rights." He therefore supported rights without regard to race or gender or social status.

His religious faith not only lay at the root of his reform efforts but also prompted him to promote the beginning of the Sunday school movement in the United States, which had been started by Robert Raikes in England. He was also the founder of America's first Bible society—an organization in Philadelphia that produced America's first mass-produced (or stereotyped) Bible. Dr. Rush was an outspoken Christian and a diligent student of the Bible, and the teachings of Scripture regularly spurred him to acts of compassion.

Compassionate Reformer

As an educational reformer, Dr. Rush started five colleges and universities. He also pioneered educational opportunities for women and supported free public schools for all youth. Regardless of the educational endeavor, his philosophy was consistent in each. His philosophy, in his own words, was "The only foundation for a useful education in a republic is to be laid in religion. Without this there can be no virtue,

and without virtue there can be no liberty, and liberty is the object and life of all republican governments." Consequently, all his educational efforts promoted religious and moral principles, as well as academic knowledge.

Dr. Rush also vigorously opposed slavery; in fact, he joined with fellow Founding Father Benjamin Franklin to organize America's first antislavery society. His position on this issue was unequivocal: "Let not our united republics be stained with the importation of a single African slave into America." Dr. Rush lobbied not only other states to outlaw the slave trade but other nations as well. He once urged a friend in Great Britain, "Fill your newspapers with essays and anecdotes of the injustice and cruelty of the African trade." Dr. Rush believed that slavery violated the principles of equality taught by Christianity. He therefore worked not only to end slavery but also to give African-Americans more opportunities. He worked alongside leaders such as Richard Allen and Absalom Jones to build the first African-American church in Philadelphia and to found America's first African-American denomination, the AME Church.

Dr. Rush spoke highly of his wife, Julia Stockton Rush, in his memoir: "Let me here bear testimony to the worth of this excellent woman. She fulfilled every duty . . . with fidelity and integrity. To me she was always a sincere and honest friend; had I yielded to her advice upon many occasions, I should have known less distress from various causes in my journey through life. . . . May God reward and bless her with an easy and peaceful old age if she should survive me, and after death confer upon her immediate and eternal happiness!"

Compassionate Peacemaker

Dr. Rush served as a member of Congress; he also remained active in politics and government long after he had signed the Declaration of Independence. Yet he successfully avoided the partisan politics that had divided his friends John Adams and Thomas Jefferson. Rush was appointed as treasurer of the United States Mint for three different U.S. presidents, each of whom was from a different political party. When asked about his own party affiliation, Dr. Rush replied, "I am neither an Aristocrat nor a Democrat. I am a Christ-ocrat." Because he considered what was godly and right to be more important than any political party, he was able to help Adams and Jefferson resolve the conflict that had destroyed their relationship for so many years.

The friendships Rush maintained with both Adams and Jefferson placed him in a unique position. He determined to risk these friendships in order to bring the two men together. He bridged the gap between the statesmen in the following ways:

1. **He placed himself in the middle between his two friends.**

2. **He pointed out their areas of agreement and previous achievements together.**

3. **He expressed confidence that they would do the right thing.**

4. **He followed up with both his friends, extending compassion and encouraging them to restore their relationship.**

Sometimes negotiating peace restores relationships between individuals; sometimes it reestablishes harmony between countries and even prevents war. Although Benjamin Rush supported the Revolutionary cause, he was not a warmonger. He often addressed the evils of war and proposed the creation of a federal office for a secretary of peace (after all, America had a secretary of war, so why not a secretary of peace?). What motivated this proposal? Personal experience; for he had personally witnessed the brutality of war: As a surgeon during the Revolution, Rush had treated serious injuries without the help of anesthesia or antiseptics. He loved life and admired the intricacies of the physical body, which he believed God had created and which he hated to see destroyed. Dr. Rush valued peace, but when necessary, he fought willingly for justice. The compassion Dr. Benjamin Rush extended to others profoundly influenced this country during his lifetime, and his ideas from two centuries ago still benefit citizens today.

1. Name three issues Dr. Benjamin Rush sought to improve or reform.

Dr. Rush addressed a broad range of issues, including medical treatments, mental health, educational reform, the abolition of slavery, prison conditions, religious expression, taxation without representation, and American independence from Great Britain.

2. How did Dr. Rush respond when he saw unfair treatment of another person? Why do you think he responded as he did?

Dr. Rush noticed when people were treated unfairly, and he consistently stood for social justice. Sometimes he wrote about the unfair treatment; other times he took direct action to provide relief. He also encouraged others to become involved in achieving social justice. His Christian faith and his compassionate character were the foundations for his advocacy.

3. What was Rush's philosophy about education in a republic? On the chart below, label each side of the triangle with one of the three components he believed necessary for effective education.

Rush considered religion to be the foundation of education. Virtue resulted from religion, and without virtue there could be no liberty.

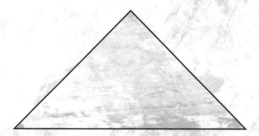

Stop and Ponder (for Group Discussion)

⚙ **Which of Dr. Rush's traits would you like your own life to reflect? Tell about one practical thing you can do this week to work toward that goal.**

⚙ **How do you respond when you see an underdog—someone in need of an advocate?**

You're in the Driver's Seat
Solving Problems

The need for mediation and problem-solving skills is not limited to Benjamin Rush's world. The U.S. secretary of state frequently uses problem-solving skills to negotiate solutions to tense global situations. Often when conflicts arise in businesses, negotiators find solutions between different groups, such as the management and labor unions. Sometimes when a conflict arises between family members or friends, someone informally mediates the situation.

Solving problems and making careful decisions are useful skills for citizens living in a democratic society. Consider the following steps for making decisions and solving problems:

1. **Identify the problem.**

2. **Gather information.**

3. **List your options.**

4. **Consider the advantages and disadvantages of each option.**

5. **Consult with people you respect to get their insights on the situation.**

6. **Make a decision.**

7. **Evaluate whether the solution worked.**

Form groups, as assigned by your teacher. In your group, identify a problem. (You can use the newspaper or the Internet to identify a problem, or you can choose a problem that affects you personally.) Using the steps listed above, try to find a solution. Present the dilemma and your solution to the class through music, art, poetry, or creative drama.

Worldview
Sociology: What are the foundational institutions for society?

As a physician, Dr. Benjamin Rush checked his patient's vital signs to help determine the client's condition; then he made a diagnosis and prescribed a treatment. Dr. Rush also observed the "vital signs" of

his culture and suggested ways to improve many social institutions.

The following are some of the causes Rush fought to improve or change:

____ **Developments in medicine**

____ **Freedom from British rule**

____ **Advancements in mental health**

____ **Advocacy for the poor**

____ **Abolition of slavery**

____ **Establishment of colleges and universities**

____ **Prison reform**

____ **Educational opportunities for women**

____ **Sunday school movement**

____ **Establishment of a Bible society**

If you had to rank these causes in order of importance, based on your own priorities, how would you do it? Put a number in each blank, with *1* indicating "most important."

What would you consider to be the most serious social injustices in the world today?

The connection between Dr. Benjamin Rush's worldview and his view of society is obvious: He lived out his Christian faith through social action. He believed that government plays a significant role in maintaining order and administering justice, so he influenced society and worked with others to change it for the better through strengthening and reforming foundational institutions.

Map Your Way

"Patriotism is both a moral and a religious duty. It includes not only the love of our neighbors but of the present and of future generations."
Benjamin Rush

Before you are ready to put your key in the ignition and drive away on your journey, take another look at those words by Benjamin Rush (above) and think carefully about the following questions:

⊚ **What do you do when you see something unjust?**

⊚ **Are your actions consistent with what you really believe?**

DVD Reflection

Watch the DVD segment for Lesson 3 and complete the following activities:

Dr. Benjamin Rush
Father of American Medicine

Three gutsy stands Dr. Rush took on behalf of the underdog:

1.

2.

3.

Label Rush used to describe himself:

> **"** I am neither an
> Aristocrat nor a Democrat.
> I am a **Christ-ocrat"**

How this identity impacted his life:

The Christian faith of Dr. Benjamin Rush led to social action.

Label you could use to describe yourself:

> **"**
>
> **"**

How this identity impacts your life:

51

For Further Study

Historical Context

Women's rights in colonial America
Yellow fever epidemic (1793)
Paine's *Common Sense*
Federalists
Anti-Federalists
Antislavery movement
AME Church

Significant Individuals and Groups

John Adams
Thomas Jefferson
Aaron Burr
Alexander Hamilton
Richard Allen
Absalom Jones

Terms

mantra
social justice
yellow fever
apprentice
bloodletting
alkali
tartar emetic
lockjaw
malady
stonewalled
reconciliation
private sector
candidate forums
stereotype
warmonger
secretary of state

Additional Resources

Lester J. Cappon, *The Adams-Jefferson Letters: The Complete Correspondence between Thomas Jefferson and Abigail and John Adams* (Chapel Hill: The University of North Carolina Press, 1988). This resource provides the text of actual correspondence between Thomas Jefferson and John Adams, offering insight into Benjamin Rush's role as a peacemaker.

Jefferson & Adams (a stage play on DVD). This dramatized portrayal of the interactions between Thomas Jefferson and John Adams can be ordered from Williamsburg Marketplace at http://www.williamsburgmarketplace.com or 800-446-9240.

David Barton, *Benjamin Rush: Signer of the Declaration of Independence* (Aledo, Tex.: WallBuilder Press, 1999). This biography of Benjamin Rush provides a thorough account of the American hero's political, medical, and spiritual contributions to our nation.

Lesson 4

NCSS Curriculum Standards

I. Culture

How do belief systems, such as religion or political ideals, influence culture?

X. Civic Ideals and Practices

How has the meaning of citizenship evolved, and what is the balance between rights and responsibilities?

VI. Power, Authority, and Governance

How are governments created, structured, and changed?

IV. Individual Development and Identity

Why do people behave as they do, and how do individuals develop from youth to adulthood?

II. Time, Continuity, and Change

What happened in the past, and how am I connected to those in the past?

Performance Expectations

Students will be able to:

1. Identify the values and virtues of George Washington, and describe ways his beliefs and attitudes helped shape our country.

2. Identify and explain the role George Washington played in influencing and shaping public policy and decision making.

3. Analyze and explain ideas and governmental mechanisms to meet needs and wants of citizens, manage conflict, and establish order and security.

4. Relate personal changes to social, cultural, and historical contexts.

5. Use knowledge of facts and concepts drawn from history to inform decision making about taking action on issues.

Lesson 4:
George Washington

Questions to Ask Yourself throughout This Unit

- What attributes set George Washington apart from other leaders during the crucial founding years of the nation and led others to honor him as a national hero?

- What is meant by Washington's distinguished title "father of his country"?

- What lasting contributions did George Washington make to the United States?

Fasten Your Seat Belt

When George Washington was elected president, there was a king in France, a czarina in Russia, an emperor in China, and a shogun in Japan. Now, more than two hundred years later, only the office of president remains. As the first American president, Washington has certainly had a lasting impact: The U.S. capital, one state, thirty-one counties, and seventeen cities (possibly eighteen, if you count George, in Washington State) are named after him. So what made this man such a historical standout?

George Washington filled many important roles that set a precedent for the leadership of this nation. He served as the commander in chief of the Continental Army, accepting the challenge of making ragtag volunteers into an effective army. He trained soldiers with perseverance and courage; he knew when to retreat and when to fight. Soldiers respected and followed him.

George Washington presided over the Constitutional Convention, serving his country by protecting freedom through the rule of law. He influenced others with his commitment to truth and self-control, knowing when to lead and when to follow. Statesmen admired and honored him.

"I am still determined to be cheerful and happy, in whatever situation I may be; for I have also learned from experience that the greater part of our happiness or misery depends upon our dispositions, and not upon our circumstances."
Martha Washington, first First Lady

George Washington served as the first president of the United States of America, sacrificing the personal leisure of retirement to accept the post from a sense of duty. He inspired Americans through his patriotism and integrity, knowing when to listen and when to act. Citizens esteemed and trusted him.

At his funeral, Henry Lee, one of George Washington's fellow Patriots, described him as "first in war, first in peace, and first in the hearts of his countrymen." Washington is rightfully called the "father of his country."

A Look in the Rearview Mirror
Washington's Journal

It was a cold autumn night, long before our nation was born, and twenty-one-year-old surveyor George Washington had a job to do. On October 31, 1753, he embarked on an official governmental mission assigned him by an English governor—a mission that would take him over a thousand miles on foot and horseback. He recruited seven others to travel with him, gathered the necessary provisions, and began his journey.

The document Washington carried could determine the future of much of the land west of the Appalachian Mountains. England and France both claimed the territory, and a disagreement was growing between them; Virginia's governor Dinwiddie therefore decided to file a diplomatic objection with the French commander at Camp Erie, General St. Pierre. Governor Dinwiddie selected Washington to deliver this important document demanding that the French leave the land.

"My mother [Mary Ball Washington] was the most beautiful woman I ever saw. All I am I owe to my mother. I attribute all my success in life to the moral, intellectual, and physical education I received from her."
George Washington

Rain and snow fell on Washington and his companions almost constantly as they traveled to confront the French commander. During the trip, Washington met with friendly Native Americans, giving them strings of wampum and twills of tobacco. The English and French competed for friendship with the natives in the region, and Washington hoped he could persuade them to partner with the English. Tanacharison of the Southern Huron tribe (or "Chief Half King," as Washington called him) described for Washington the offensive treatment the Hurons had received from the French. He told Washington about the way the French had broken treaties with them and about his plan therefore to officially abolish ties with France. After lengthy discussions, Washington convinced Half King and four other Native American leaders to accompany him on the trip to meet the French.

As they traveled, Washington watched for prime sites for future English forts and settlements. Despite harsh weather conditions, they finally reached the French fort where Washington presented to the French commander the official demand to leave the area. While waiting for a response, Washington gathered useful information about the numbers of the French and their weapon supplies. Meanwhile, the French tried to persuade Half King to maintain ties with them and even offered him bribes of weapons and liquor, but Half King refused. In the end, the objection Washington delivered was unsuccessful. The French sent Washington home with their written response to the Virginia governor, refusing to relinquish the French claims to the disputed land.

Washington prepared to return to Virginia, but the winter weather had gotten much worse and much colder. He knew it was crucial to carry back the response from the French as quickly as possible, but the horses were weak from the long journey, and the supplies were low. So Washington and his guide, Christopher Gist, decided to leave the rest of the group and take the shortest route home, traveling through the woods on foot and leaving the others to return at a slower pace.

On their return trip, a party of Native Americans ambushed the two, firing a shot that barely missed. Washington and Gist eluded that initial attack and then traveled throughout the night and all the next day in hopes of losing their foes. Finally reaching the river, they were dismayed to see it hadn't completely frozen yet, so they could not walk across. Ice floes drifted in some parts of the freezing river, and in other places, even though ice covered the river, the ice was still too thin to walk on. They began to build a raft—a project that required a full day.

After sunset, they finally launched into the icy waters. But the raft was quickly dashed into an ice jam, threatening to sink the small craft. Attempting to stabilize the raft, Washington thrust his push pole into the river, but the raging water seized the pole, knocking Washington off balance and pulling him overboard into the icy river. Grasping one of the raft logs, Washington was able to save himself. But despite their best efforts, he and Gist were unable to navigate the raft toward either shore. The two finally managed to guide the raft to a small island in the river, where they endured a cold, wet, miserable night. In fact, Gist's fingers and toes froze in the extreme weather. Fortunately, by the next morning the river was frozen solid enough for the two men to walk across to the other side and continue their excursion. Washington finally arrived back in Williamsburg and relayed the French response.

Washington's dangerous journey had lasted eleven weeks. During the harrowing trek, Washington had kept a daily journal. Some weeks after his return, the *Maryland Gazette* published his journal. Respect for the young surveyor grew as a result of the courage and perseverance he displayed on that trip.

1. George Washington earned considerable respect because of his actions during this assignment. List three accomplishments he made during the journey.

Washington's negotiations with the Native Americans won friendships for the English. Using his astute observation skills, he identified prime sites for future English developments and gathered useful information about the enemy's strength in number and weaponry. He managed to traverse long stretches of wilderness in hazardous conditions and complete his task in a relatively short time. He used numerous skills of a competent frontiersman, such as the ability to build a raft, in order to complete the job he had undertaken.

2. How do you think the publishing of his journal in the *Maryland Gazette* helped Washington?

Because his journals were read by many of the colonists, he gained widespread respect.

3. Identify two character traits Washington exhibited during this trip, and give two examples or illustrations from the text to back up each one.

Students' answers may focus on Washington's persuasive abilities, peacemaking skills, observation skills, strength of character, professionalism, dedication, decisiveness, courage, perseverance, loyalty, leadership, or creativity in problem solving.

School Zone Ahead
Newspaper (Journalism Activity)

George Washington recorded a detailed account of his journey with seven other English colonists from Virginia to Camp Erie. These journal entries were published in the *Maryland Gazette* on March 21 and 28, 1754. This primary source is available on the Internet. Now your class will publish a newspaper about the diplomatic journey from various perspectives.

In groups of two or three, as designated by your teacher, divide the following components of the newspaper. Make sure each group is assigned both written and visual projects.

Written Projects

Headline News Story (front page): Write an article to be used on the front page of your newspaper, summarizing Washington's trip. Include some of the key moments from the journey, as well as inferences about the reasons for the trip and conclusions about the value of the trip. You may want to create "quotes" that key individuals such as Washington, Gist, Chief Half King, Governor Dinwiddie, or General St. Pierre might have said.

Interview (front page): Pretend you are interviewing Christopher Gist about the raft construction and river crossing during their return trip. Write an article about the two-day river adventure Gist and Washington experienced.

Column (front page): Half King told George Washington about his meeting with the French commander, in which the French tried to bribe the Huron to side with them. Write a column from Half King's point of view about the meeting.

Insider's Briefing (middle section): Imagine that you are John Davison, an interpreter of many Native American dialects who joined Washington's band at Loggs Town, and that you were privy to the discussions with the Native Americans. Write a report comparing various arguments the tribal leaders of the Six Nations might have presented.

Real Estate Report (business section): Servitor John MacQuire also helped Washington. Imagine you are MacQuire, and you've been listening to Washington's comparison of the two sites at the fork of the Allegheny and Monongahela Rivers. After your return, Washington asks you to write a report analyzing the two sites and drawing conclusions about the best site to build a fort.

Editorial Page: The land dispute over the Ohio River Valley involved three groups of people with varying viewpoints: the Native Americans, the French, and the English colonists. Compose three different editorials, written from the viewpoint of people who represent each group.

Visual Projects

Shopping Advertisement (business section): Two traders, Henry Steward and William Jenkins, accompanied Washington on the trip. Design an advertisement for the business section of the paper that promotes commercial opportunities in the Ohio River Valley. Be sure to include information about what items Native Americans typically traded, as well as what items the English bartered with.

Real Estate Advertisement (business section): When Washington was traveling to Pennsylvania, he looked for land that could potentially be used for English forts and settlements. Create an advertisement encouraging colonists to buy these plots of land between Virginia and Pennsylvania. Be sure to include graphics as well as to describe the climate, landforms, wildlife, and reasons why people would want to settle there.

⚙️ **Weather Page:** Design a map of the Ohio River region detailing weather conditions for four consecutive days during Washington's trip. Include temperature highs and lows, a windchill chart, and precipitation amounts. You may want to use weather-related Web sites (such as www.weather.com) or an almanac to help you.

⚙️ **Map:** Create a map that traces Washington's journey from Virginia to Camp Erie. Mark and label key points or events along the way.

Historical Marker
Bulletproof George Washington

George Washington proved his bravery and determination on his diplomatic mission to Camp Erie. Two years later, he would have the chance to demonstrate that same courage—this time on the military battlefield. By 1755, it was clear that the tensions between the English and French would not be resolved except through war, so the British and Americans (who were still British citizens at the time) prepared to do battle. General Edward Braddock, commander in chief of the British forces, invited young colonel George Washington and his Virginia buckskins to join his forces, with Washington serving as General Braddock's aide.

Washington's mother was worried about him and tried to persuade her son not to accept the invitation. Washington said, "The God to whom you commended me, madam, when I set out upon a more perilous errand [to Camp Erie], defended me from all harm, and I trust He will do so now."

"Discipline is the soul of an army. It makes small numbers formidable; procures success to the weak, and esteem to all."
George Washington

As Braddock's troops marched toward the French's Fort Duquesne (now the city of Pittsburgh), Colonel Washington came down with a high fever and was ordered to drop out of the march to recuperate. After a few days, even though he was not fully recovered, Washington caught up with the troops and rejoined them. A group from the Shawnee and Delaware tribes arrived and offered to join the fight against the French. Washington urged Braddock to accept their offer, but Braddock, unacquainted with the American mode of fighting in the forests—from tree to tree and from behind rocks—rejected Washington's advice and arrogantly refused help from these tribes. Braddock planned to march his army to an open field, face the enemy head-on, impress the French and Native Americans with the size of his army, and then lead a direct attack on them. He continued to ignore warnings from both Washington and Benjamin Franklin about Native American styles of warfare, surprise attacks, and ambushes.

The 1,300 British troops, dressed in full, bright red uniforms and marching in exact rows, moved forward toward Fort Duquesne in a line that stretched almost four miles in length. The French commander, with a force of 72 French regulars, 146 Canadian militiamen, and 637 Native Americans (a combined force of 855), laid an ambush in the woods seven miles from the fort. Suddenly a storm of bullets pounded the British ranks! But not a gun was seen—the enemy was invisible. Blue smoke revealed that the shower of musket balls had come from the trees. The British soldiers fired back into the woods at unseen targets but with little effect. The Native Americans, skilled in the art of ambush and guerrilla warfare, moved from tree to tree and fired at the stationary British soldiers, whose red coats provided easy targets. The forward detachment of soldiers panicked and retreated, leaving their cannons in the hands of the French.

Braddock was furious about the mode of battle; he considered it a cowardly way to fight, yet he was a lion in combat. He continued undaunted, moving among the soldiers while being showered with bullets and having five horses shot out from under him. Both his English aides were wounded. Washington, the general's only uninjured aide, rode over every part of the field carrying out the general's orders. The pandemonium lasted over two hours. Relaying the general's orders to subordinates in all parts of the field made Washington a conspicuous mark to the enemy. One observer who was watching Washington during the battle reported, "I expected every moment to see him fall." Two horses were shot from under him and his coat was torn four times by musket balls, but he escaped without injury. As he later explained, "By the all-powerful dispensations of Providence, I have been protected beyond all human expectations."

Casualties were high, and the battle was brutal, but even though the British lost hundreds of soldiers, Braddock would not allow them to retreat. Finally, Braddock was shot and sank to the ground, wounded. With their leader down, the British turned and ran. The battle became a rout; the British abandoned everything to the enemy, even the private papers of the general.

Braddock was hurriedly carried from the field on a stretcher, and he lingered in pain for several days. A wounded aide reported that Braddock was totally silent the first day and at night said only, "Who would have thought it?" Later he said, "We shall better know how to deal with them another time." Then he died.

Out of the 1,300 British troops, 714 were shot down (only 30 of the French and Native Americans were wounded); and of the 86 British and American officers, Washington was the only officer on horseback who was not shot down. Following the battle, Native Americans testified that they had specifically singled out Washington and repeatedly shot at him many times, but he was never injured. They became convinced that an Invisible Power protected him and that no bullet could harm him, describing him as "the man who is the particular favorite of Heaven, and who can never die in battle."

1. What did Washington think of Braddock's strategy against the French? How would you explain his response to his commander's orders?

George Washington thought Braddock's battle strategy was inadequate for fighting in the frontier of North America, and he urged Braddock to accept the help of the Delaware and the Shawnee. But since Washington was serving under General Braddock's command, he obeyed his orders. Washington's deference to Braddock's orders shows his respect for Braddock's authority and position.

2. Less than ten years after this battle, George Washington joined other Patriots in declaring independence from the British and opposing them on the battlefield. What caused Washington to join in the Revolutionary cause?

Washington had gone to war with General Braddock in order to defend his country, his state, and his home. It was this same motivation that caused Washington to become a leader of the Revolutionary cause. The British had attempted to abolish the colonies' representative governments; they even attacked America to enforce their desires. Washington was willing to fight to preserve our God-given liberties and our free form of government.

3. Based on Washington's experiences and your own principles, when is it necessary to submit to authority and when is it appropriate to oppose those in leadership?

Washington understood the importance of showing respect for authority and submitting to the proper chain of command. After pointing out the risks of Braddock's plan and after Braddock disregarded Washington's advice, Washington still followed Braddock's orders even though he disagreed. Likewise, it is important for us to show respect for authority figures, such as parents, teachers, and law officers (see Romans 13:5 and Colossians 3:20). However, if there is a conflict between what an authority says and what God says, God is the higher authority (see Acts 5:29). So if government commands something that violates what God commands, we need to follow what God commands (this practice is what led, in part, to the American Revolution). Finally, when it comes to what we want to do as individuals, remember that God is higher than we are; therefore, if there is a conflict of wills, we must obey what God commands rather than what we would prefer.

Stop and Ponder (for Group Discussion)

- Have you been in a situation where you asked your parents or teachers to reconsider their plans or decisions? What was the result? Are there respectful and disrespectful ways to go about doing that? Explain.

- What rules are you expected to follow (home, community, school, etc.)? Under what circumstances would it be appropriate for you to respectfully disagree with those in authority?

Right of Way: Self-Control

Self-control means restraint of self—operating within boundaries. The opposite of self-control is excess and self-indulgence—operating without control.

How well do you manage yourself?

Self-Indulgent
act in excess; live out of control

Wishy-Washy
swayed by popular opinion; change decisions often

Self-Controlled
show restraint; live within wise boundaries

Commander in Chief

Imagine trying to train a shopkeeper unaccustomed to being outside in harsh weather how to load and fire a musket in a blizzard. Or trying to teach a fisherman who lived a solitary life on the sea as his own boss how to follow orders without question.

When George Washington became commander in chief of the Continental

Army, this was his challenge. His troops consisted of untrained, sometimes undisciplined farmers, fishermen, and merchants; and he had to train these novices to face the best-trained and greatest military power in the world at that time. Not only were Washington's men inexperienced, but they were also heavily outnumbered. British general William Howe commanded a force of thirty thousand professional British soldiers and hired fighters from Germany, while Washington's troops numbered fewer than ten thousand.

By the end of August 1776, only a few months after the American Revolution had begun, General Howe trapped General Washington and his troops on Long Island. Fierce fighting began on August 27, and by August 29 Washington faced disaster. Howe planned to attack and destroy the Americans the following morning, expecting an easy victory. However, in the intervening hours while the unsuspecting Howe was preparing for the assault, Washington gathered every boat available, from fishing boats to rowboats, and ferried his troops off of Long Island and across the East River during the night. At sunrise, many of the Patriot troops still had not been moved off the island, but a dense fog moved in and not only prevented the British from attacking but also allowed the remaining Americans to escape. Major Ben Tallmadge, Washington's chief of intelligence, wrote,

As the dawn of the next day approached, those of us who remained in the trenches became very anxious for our own safety, and when the dawn appeared there were several regiments still on duty. At this time a very dense fog began to rise, and it seemed to settle in a peculiar manner over both encampments. I recollect this peculiar Providential occurrence perfectly well, and so very dense was the atmosphere that I could scarcely discern a man at six yards distance.

By means of this "Providential occurrence," the entire American army was preserved and was able to continue their fight against the British until they finally won.

The Revolution continued for eight long years, and as it turned out, trapping the Americans on Long Island was the best opportunity the British had to defeat them. But General Washington's skillful maneuvering and strategic retreat and a providential intervention saved the Continental Army. Washington soon shifted the battle's momentum and crossed the Delaware River with his troops on December 26, 1776, winning a decisive victory over the German mercenaries at the famous Battle of Trenton. The self-control of George Washington was an example to his men, helping them know when to retreat and when to fight. This wisdom characterized Washington's leadership throughout the Revolution, finally resulting in complete victory and independence from the British.

President of the Constitutional Convention

The sun beat down on the city of Philadelphia in the summer of 1787. Fifty-five of America's most respected leaders had gathered there to discuss creating a new government. Before the Revolution, Americans had been governed by the British, but during the Revolution they had created their own government under the Articles of Confederation. They soon found that this form of government was too weak to handle many of the difficulties they faced, so they now agreed that they needed to strengthen the government under which they were operating or create a new one.

The latter option was chosen, but there would be many difficulties because of the different interests represented by the delegates. Who could the delegates trust to guide the proceedings fairly? They unanimously elected George Washington, who was dressed in his striking general's uniform, as president of the Constitutional Convention, and for the next four months, the delegates intensely debated volatile issues such as slavery, fair representation, state's rights, and governmental checks and balances under Washington's evenhanded leadership.

Washington's quiet and dignified presence set the tone for the proceedings. He rarely spoke, but his leadership, prestige, and authority were key to the success of the convention. In a letter to Thomas Jefferson, James Monroe wrote, "Be assured [Washington's] influence carried this government." Washington knew when to listen and when to speak.

Since Washington was president at the time of the convention deliberations, he did not speak on the nature of the executive office (the presidency), but he did cast his vote along with the other members of his Virginia delegation. He voted for a single executive (some had suggested more than one, or even a council), and he voted for requiring a three-fourths congressional majority to override a president instead of the two-thirds margin that eventually passed and is still the policy today.

President of the United Thirteen Colonies

When George Washington was unanimously elected as the first president of the new republic, people debated whether to call him "His Highness" (the British custom, stemming from the distinction for kings and queens) or "His Excellency" (the title Americans used to address state governors). There were even some who wanted to make the new president a monarch—a king. Washington understood that each of his actions as the nation's first president would set a precedent not only for the new country but also for presidents after him. (As modern historian Garry Wills noted, "Others will sit in his chair and do what he has done. The same authority will be wielded, the same limits observed.") Understanding the importance of his every action, Washington flatly refused to be considered a king and even directly rebuked those who suggested it. He chose the title "Mr. President," thus clarifying that his office was different from that of a king or a governor. Washington understood what was best for Americans. John Adams, who was elected vice president under Washington, wrote, "I glory in the character of Washington because I know him to be an exemplification of the American character."

Washington's character was also revealed in his selection of cabinet members. Understanding the importance of unity in the new nation, and realizing the value of differing opinions, Washington intentionally selected cabinet members of diverse viewpoints who represented different movements in America, including Alexander Hamilton (secretary of the treasury) and Thomas Jefferson (secretary of state), who were fierce opponents of each other.

Washington understood the benefits of self-control, knowing when to listen and when to act. He worked for unity and inspired Americans through integrity and patriotism. He set the standard for what it means to be the president of the United States.

1. Think about two of George Washington's significant actions or decisions. In the chart below, write them in the appropriate column

for how much self-control each demonstrated. One example has been done for you.

2. Choose another leader (from the United States or another country), and plot one of his or her actions on the chart below. An example is shown.

3. Think about some of your own actions over the past week. Plot out two of them on the chart below. How well do you manage yourself?

Self-Indulgent	Wishy-Washy	Self-Controlled
		Washington kept quiet about his views on the executive office during the Constitutional Convention.
Ron Artest, an NBA basketball player, got into a fight with fans in Detroit in 2004.		

You're in the Driver's Seat
Exercising Self-Control

As he was growing up, George Washington had many opportunities to be self-indulgent—to join in his friends' poor decisions, to act impulsively, or to behave in ways he'd regret later. To help develop self-control when he was a teenager, Washington copied a list of 110 rules, based on behavior guidelines created by Jesuits in the 1500s. His list included some of the following rules. Read the rules carefully (along with the modern-day translations), and rate how effectively you follow each one.

1. Every action done ought to be with some sign of respect to those that are present.

    Do your actions show respect for those around you?

NEVER		SOMETIMES		ALWAYS
1	2	3	4	5

22. Show not yourself glad at the misfortune of another.

    Do you offer empathy when someone else is going through a hard time?

NEVER		SOMETIMES		ALWAYS
1	2	3	4	5

49. Use no reproachful language against anyone, neither curse nor revile.

    Do your words build people up, not tear them down?

NEVER		SOMETIMES		ALWAYS
1	2	3	4	5

56. It is better to be alone than in bad company.

    Do you choose your friends wisely?

NEVER		SOMETIMES		ALWAYS
1	2	3	4	5

108(a). When you speak of God or His attributes, let it be seriously and with reverence.

    Does your attitude toward God show respect for his holiness?

NEVER		SOMETIMES		ALWAYS
1	2	3	4	5

108(b). Honor and obey your natural parents, although they be poor.

    Do you listen to and honor your parents?

NEVER		SOMETIMES		ALWAYS
1	2	3	4	5

109. Let your recreations be . . . not sinful.

    Do you avoid wrong behavior during your free time?

NEVER		SOMETIMES		ALWAYS
1	2	3	4	5

110. Labor to keep alive . . . that little spark of [heavenly] fire called conscience.

    Do you listen to your internal sense of right and wrong?

NEVER		SOMETIMES		ALWAYS
1	2	3	4	5

Worldview

Politics: What Is the Best Type of Government?

Washington was known as a man of prayer, and he believed that God answered his prayers. In his inaugural address, he said, "The propitious smiles of Heaven can never be expected on a nation that disregards the eternal rules of order and right which Heaven itself has ordained." In his Farewell Address, he reiterated the importance of religion and morality as the only foundations for continued success in American government.

Washington, as well as most of our country's Founders, clearly believed that God intervenes in the affairs of humankind, and he considered religion essential for a moral society. In describing the citizens of his country, he said, "With slight shades of difference, you have the same religion, manners, habits and political principles."

The government designed by the Founding Fathers reflects the following Christian beliefs: (1) people are created in the image of God and have certain God-given rights; and (2) humans have a fallen nature and a natural tendency to depravity (a sinful/corrupt state). On the basis of the first belief, they established a government that balanced the need for an ordered society with protection for the God-given rights of every individual. The system of checks and balances in our government was created based on this second belief. The Founders truly looked—as Washington said—to "the eternal rules of order and right which Heaven itself has ordained" as their guide.

Map Your Way

"By the all-powerful dispensations of Providence, I have been protected beyond all human probability or expectation; for I had four bullets through my coat, and two horses shot under me, yet escaped unhurt, although death was leveling my companions on every side of me."
George Washington

Some historians describe George Washington as a Deist (see diagram below). How does the quote above by Washington himself, as well as other information you have learned about him, prove otherwise?

Before you proceed on your way, consider:

- **Would you fit somewhere on this diagram?**

- **Do you think God is real?**

- **If so, does he have a role in your day-to-day life?**

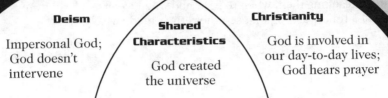

Deism

Impersonal God;
God doesn't
intervene

**Shared
Characteristics**

God created
the universe

Christianity

God is involved in
our day-to-day lives;
God hears prayer

DVD Reflection

Watch the DVD segment for Lesson 4 and complete the following activities:

George Washington
Bulletproof President

Dave Stotts says, "The self-control of George Washington was an example to his men, teaching them when to fight and when to retreat." Give an example of a time Washington used the retreat tactic wisely.

Briefly describe two times when Washington survived seemingly insurmountable odds:

Why do you think the DVD segment describes Washington as a prototype?

For Further Study

Geography

Washington's journey from Virginia
to Camp Erie in Pennsylvania
Fort Duquesne (now Pittsburgh)
Long Island, New York
East River
Delaware River

Historical Context

Continental Army
Constitutional Convention
French-English relations
in the mid-1700s
Native American–English
relations in the mid-1700s
Battle of Trenton
Articles of Confederation

Significant Individuals and Groups

Governor Dinwiddie
General St. Pierre
Chief Half King
Huron tribe
Christopher Gist
John Davison
Six Nations
Edward Braddock
Shawnee tribe
Delaware tribe
General William Howe
Ben Tallmadge
Martha Washington
Mary Ball Washington
Jesuits

Terms

surveyor
diplomatic objection
wampum
servitor
buckskins
regulars
militiamen
rout

Additional Resources

David Barton, *The Bulletproof George Washington* (Aledo, Tex.: WallBuilder Press, 1990). This short book focuses on Washington's bravery in the French and Indian War battle at Monongahela, as well as his gratitude to God for his protection.

M. E. Bradford, *A Worthy Company: Brief Lives of the Framers of the United States Constitution* (Plymouth, Mass.: Plymouth Rock Foundation, 1982). Bradford's research unveils the crucial role Christian statesmen played in the founding of the United States.

David McCullough, *1776* (New York: Simon & Schuster, 2005). This book tells the story of General George Washington and the American soldiers he led.

Lesson 5

NCSS Curriculum Standards

I. Culture

How do belief systems, such as religion or political ideals, influence culture?

II. Time, Continuity, and Change

What happened in the past, and how am I connected to those in the past?

III. People, Places, and Environments

What implications do environmental changes have for people?

IV. Individual Development and Identity

Why do people behave as they do, and how do individuals develop from youth to adulthood?

VIII. Science, Technology, and Society

What is the relationship between science and society?

IX. Global Connections

How do age-old ethnic enmities impact human rights?

Performance Expectations

Students will be able to:

1. Explain how experiences may be interpreted by people from diverse cultural perspectives.

2. Develop critical sensitivities such as empathy regarding attitudes, values, and behaviors of people in different historical contexts.

3. Describe physical system changes, such as seasons, climate, and weather.

4. Describe the ways family, ethnicity, and nationality contribute to personal identity.

5. Show through specific examples how science and technology have changed people's perceptions of the world.

6. Analyze examples of cooperation and interdependence among groups, societies, and nations.

Lesson 5:
Benjamin Banneker

Questions to Ask Yourself throughout This Unit

- What beliefs shaped Benjamin Banneker?

- What lessons can you learn from the life of Benjamin Banneker?

- What attributes helped Benjamin Banneker achieve his goals? Note the differences and similarities between George Ellicott and Benjamin Banneker.

- What are some of the advantages of cross-generational and cross-cultural relationships?

Fasten Your Seat Belt

Benjamin Banneker, a free black who lived during the founding years of our nation, had a dream. He dreamed of becoming a mathematician and a scientist someday. During this time in American history, however, an education for an African-American was nearly impossible. But Benjamin didn't let that stop him—in fact, his whole family story is bursting with dreams that came true.

"The color of the skin is in no way connected with the strength of the mind or intellectual powers."
Benjamin Banneker

As a result of his hard work and persistent pursuit of learning, Benjamin Banneker developed a variety of skills. When he was nearly sixty years old, he learned about astronomy and how to use the scientific instruments of a surveyor. Through a network of friends, he was selected to help survey the land for the new Federal District, which is now Washington DC. His work secured a place for him in American history.

Despite facing many prejudices during the time he lived, Benjamin Banneker did not let his race or age hinder his pursuit of knowledge. His example provides important lessons for the rest of us as we face our own obstacles and challenges.

A Look in the Rearview Mirror
A Legacy of Dreams

Molly Walsh was Benjamin Banneker's grandmother. While working as a dairymaid in her native England, Molly accidentally tipped over a bucket of milk. Since the milk was lost to the master, he accused her of stealing the milk—a crime punishable by death. In courts in England at the time, if an accused criminal demonstrated the ability to read, his or her sentence could be reduced. So Molly requested a Bible and read from it to the court. This practice was termed "calling for the book," and it literally saved her life. So instead of executing Molly, the authorities sent her to the British colonies in America as an indentured servant. In 1698, when she arrived in America, Molly was much like a slave. For seven years she worked on a tobacco plantation, where she learned the art of tobacco farming—one of the largest and most prosperous agricultural pursuits in the colonies at that time. She envisioned owning her own tobacco farm someday and worked diligently to make that dream come true.

After seven years, Molly earned her freedom. Then she rented a plot of property in a beautiful river valley in Maryland and cleared enough land to grow a garden and a tobacco crop. Even though she opposed slavery, she felt she had no choice but to buy two strong, hardworking slaves. One, called Bannka, claimed to be the son of an African king. The men helped Molly build a house and raise tobacco before she freed them. Eventually she married Bannka and took his name. Their first daughter, Mary, also married an African slave, named Robert. Robert gained his freedom, converted to Christianity, and took his wife's family name of Bannka, which was eventually changed to Banneker. Robert and Mary named their firstborn son Benjamin.

> *"Evil communication corrupts good manners. I hope to live to hear that good communication corrects bad manners."*
> **Benjamin Banneker**

Robert Banneker, like Molly, dreamed of owning his own land, for he believed that owning land made the difference between independence and slavery. So Benjamin's parents worked hard and harvested and sold seven thousand pounds of tobacco so they could buy one hundred acres of land next to Molly's farm. The deed listed both the father, Robert, and the son, Benjamin, as the owners, so Benjamin legally owned property in the Patapsco River Valley when he was only six years old. He weeded the tobacco, he hoed the corn, he tended the cows, but in his spare time, he hurried to his grandmother's farm, where she taught him to read and write using her most treasured book, the huge family Bible. Benjamin remembered every detail and soon learned all that Molly could teach him, so Molly arranged for him to attend a one-room Quaker school. While African-Americans were rarely allowed to receive an education, the Quakers—a denomination of Christians—advocated equal treatment for African-Americans in all areas, including education.

One of Benjamin's classmates later recalled that Benjamin dived into his books—he thirsted for information. School lasted only a few months each year in his day, but Benjamin craved more. Of course, in his world, there was no Internet—he didn't even have a library! So he watched and studied everything. He observed the habits of wildlife, he calculated thirty-six separate steps in growing tobacco, and he studied the stars. He also pursued mathematics and concentrated on understanding the mechanics of motion and machinery. His brain growled with insatiable hunger, and step by step Benjamin Banneker investigated the world around him.

When Banneker was twenty-one years old, he dreamed of building a clock. Clocks were somewhat rare in colonial Maryland, but Benjamin managed to borrow a pocket watch so he could study it. He noted every detail and remembered the workings of the watch precisely enough to construct drawings of the interior. He then calculated the size of the various wheels and gears and meticulously carved a replica of each from pieces of wood. He labored diligently on every part and then added a bell that struck on the hour. To Banneker's great delight, that clock kept time accurately for more than fifty years. The clock amazed his neighbors, and as word of his scientific achievements spread, he welcomed many visitors who trekked to his cabin to see his remarkable workmanship.

Benjamin Banneker was an avid learner on a wide range of topics. He heeded the admonition he had no doubt learned from his grandmother's Bible: to apply his heart to knowledge (Proverbs 22:17)—and he did so with all his heart. Minute after minute, step after step, year after year, Benjamin faithfully examined the world around him. After his father died, the farm required even more of his time, so he sacrificed sleep to continue his scholarly pursuits. As he grew older, his desire to learn only increased. Eventually he was able to purchase his first book—a Bible—and he also obtained a flute and violin; he wanted to learn about everything.

1. One of the common dreams that motivated Molly Walsh, Robert Banneker, and Benjamin Banneker was the desire for freedom of some sort. What kind of freedom was each of them looking to achieve?

In addition to the desire to own their own property and belongings, they all wanted freedom: Molly Walsh wanted freedom from being an indentured servant, as well as freedom from the death penalty; Robert Banneker wanted freedom from slavery; and Benjamin Banneker wanted the freedom to learn.

2. What obstacles did each face, and how did they overcome these obstacles?

Molly Walsh overcame the death sentence issued against her by proving

she could read. Then she overcame her status as a lowly servant by working hard and saving money to start a successful farming business. Robert Banneker believed that owning land assured independence, so he worked hard, saved money, and bought land for a farm. Benjamin Banneker overcame prejudice and limited educational opportunities by learning as much as he could through his grandmother's instruction, the Quaker school, and his careful observations of the world around him.

Stop and Ponder (for Group Discussion)

What obstacles hinder your ability to learn? What advantages do you have that Benjamin Banneker and his family lacked?

Compare the way you view learning to the way Benjamin Banneker looked at learning. What can you learn from his life about how to maximize learning opportunities?

School Zone Ahead
Word Problems (Math Activity)

Math puzzles fascinated Benjamin Banneker. He jotted down equations and math problems in his manuscript journal. See if you can work some of his actual math problems below, which Benjamin taught himself to solve. (His studies at the Quaker school had offered him only the basics.)

1. A Triangle Puzzle
   Suppose a ladder 60 feet long is to be placed in a street so as to reach a window 37 feet high on one side of the street, and without moving the bottom, it will reach another window on the other side of the street which is 23 feet high. What is the breadth of the street?

(Hint: You may need to use the Pythagorean theorem: $a^2 + b^2 = c^2$.)

The answer to this problem is 102.6 feet. The problem can be solved by constructing two right triangles. Sides of the first triangle are 37, 60, and x. Sides of the second triangle are 23, 60, and y. The hypotenuse for each triangle is 60. Apply Pythagorean theorem, which says that the sum of the squares of the sides of a right triangle are equal to the square of the hypotenuse. Then add the length of x and y to determine the width of the street: $x + y = 102.6$.

2. A Livestock Puzzle
   A gentleman sent his servant with £100 to buy 100 cattle, with orders to pay £5 for each bullock, 20 shillings for each cow, and one shilling for each sheep. What number of each sort did he bring to his master? (Hint: The symbol £ stands for British pounds. Also, 20 shillings equal one pound.)

Answer: 100 cows at one £ each = 100 £. He bought only the 100 cows his master requested, and 100 cows at one £ each = 100 £. There would have been no money left over for bullocks or sheep.

Many people living in America during the eighteenth and nineteenth centuries had only an eighth-grade education, but an eighth-grade education in earlier years was much more rigorous than what it is today. Check out these problems from an eighth-grade final exam from Salina, Kansas, in 1895.

3. Wheat Price
   If a load of wheat weighs 3,942 pounds, what is it worth at 50 cents per bushel, deducting 1,050 pounds for tare (weight of the empty vehicle)? (Assume that one bushel of wheat weighs 60 pounds.)

The answer is $24.10. The total weight of the wheat (2,892) is determined by subtracting the tare weight from the total weight. Divide the difference by 60 to determine the number of bushels and multiply that number by $0.50 to determine the total value of the wheat.

4. Lumber Price

What is the cost of 40 boards that are 12 inches wide and 16 feet long, at $20 per square meter? (Hint: One foot equals .3048 meters.)

The answer is $1,189.16. The square meters is found by multiplying 16 by .3048 (length), times .3048 (width). The square meters times the number of boards (40), times the number of dollars per meter (20) equals $1,189.16

5. Land Price

At $15 per acre, what is the cost of a farm that is 640 rods long on each side? (Hint: One acre equals 160 square rods.)

The answer is $38,400. One acre equals 160 square rods. The farm is a square, 640 rods per side. To determine the total square rods of the farm, multiply 640 times 640. To calculate the number of acres in the farm, divide the total number of square rods (409,600) by 160. Then multiply the total number of acres by $15 to determine the total cost of the farm.

Historical Marker

Surveying the New Capital City, Washington DC

In February 1791, a portly George Ellicott and a trim Benjamin Banneker mounted packhorses and headed to the Federal Territory. This was the beginning of a long journey that would result in the foundations of our nation's capital. But the journey of friendship between the two had begun much earlier.

In the first four decades of his life, in the solitude of his tobacco farm, Benjamin Banneker had managed to learn much by studying on his own. But

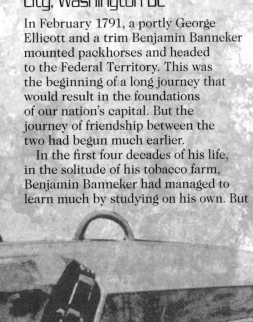

in the early 1770s, Benjamin's world began to grow wider when a new family, the Ellicotts, moved to the valley and built a mill near the Banneker farm. The Ellicotts were enterprising Quakers with a clear vision for success. A thriving community grew up around their mills, and suddenly Benjamin Banneker was linked with a new world outside his farm.

A unique friendship was forged between the forty-seven-year-old Benjamin Banneker and the eighteen-year-old George Ellicott. Common interests, particularly a fascination with astronomy, bridged their differences in age, race, and social standing. Ten years later, when Banneker was fifty-seven years old, his twenty-eight-year-old friend George loaned the older man astronomy books, a telescope, drafting instruments, and a drop-leaf table. Banneker marveled at the night sky as he peered through the borrowed telescope. Utilizing his understanding of complex mathematical concepts, along with a simple compass and ruler, he constructed astrological projections of solar and lunar eclipses. Consumed with curiosity, he embarked on a new hobby: astronomy.

Banneker pursued astronomy with an intense focus. Eagerly awaiting each night, he measured celestial movements with precision and hoped to calculate an ephemeris—daily astronomical tables—to be put into an almanac he was writing. During colonial times, almanacs were indispensable best sellers, second only to the Bible in importance. Navigators used almanacs to calculate their positions on the seas; farmers relied on almanacs for weather forecasts and planting times; and almanacs also served as calendars, with entertaining stories and useful instruction sprinkled throughout. Banneker mentioned the possibility of publishing his own almanac to his friend George Ellicott, who encouraged him to undertake the project. Ellicott's support boosted Banneker's confidence, and he pushed himself to achieve his dream.

Banneker's passion for his work is obvious from this description, recorded by George Ellicott's granddaughter of her mother's visit to Banneker's cabin:

His door stood wide open, and so closely was his mind engaged that they entered without being seen. Immediately upon observing them he arose and with much courtesy invited them to be seated. The large oval table at which Banneker sat was strewn with works on astronomy and with scientific appurtenances [equipment]. He alluded to his love of the study of

astronomy and mathematics as quite unsuited to a man of his class, and regretted his slow advancement in them, owing to the laborious nature of his agricultural engagements, which obliged him to spend the greater portion of his time in the fields.

As the aging Banneker searched for a publisher for his almanac, he experienced many rejections. But while waiting for favorable responses from publishers, an astonishing opportunity came to him.

"Presumption should never make us neglect that which appears easy to us, nor despair make us lose courage at the sight of difficulties."
Benjamin Banneker

President George Washington had chosen a site for the capital of the new republic, and Major Andrew Ellicott was appointed to conduct the survey for the federal city. Andrew Ellicott—who had lived near Banneker and was George's cousin—needed an assistant who understood astronomy and knew how to use scientific instruments. Banneker was chosen, leading Benjamin to embark on what he described as his greatest adventure. For the next three months, Banneker lived in an observation tent and maintained a vigorous schedule, working nights and catching naps during the day. He observed, calculated, and recorded notes in surveying the ten-mile-square

district that became Washington DC. Benjamin Banneker suffered from the cold and humid climate as well as from his time-consuming work, but he was able to utilize his lifetime of learning. He quickly won the respect of his coworkers. They noticed his gentleness and his neatness; they admired his faith and dignity; but most of all they recognized the accuracy of his scientific work.

1. **How did the world of Benjamin Banneker change when the Ellicott family moved to the Patapsco River valley in Maryland?**

A thriving community grew up around Banneker's previously quiet and isolated home. Banneker's neighbors offered him opportunities to make new acquaintances and to learn more about the world. In particular, he benefited from his interactions with George Ellicott, both as a friend and a colleague. In short, his world suddenly broadened, providing him more opportunity to learn.

2. **List differences and similarities in the lives of Benjamin Banneker and George Ellicott. Why do you think they became friends despite their differences?**

Ellicott was a teenager and Banneker was in his forties when they first met. Banneker was African-American and Ellicott was Caucasian. Banneker was basically self-taught, while Ellicott had been educated through the school system. Ellicott's family had greater wealth than Banneker did. Despite the many differences, the two men shared similar desires to learn, and both

had special interests in astronomy and mathematics; they also shared a common faith in God.

Stop and Ponder (for Group Discussion)

🌀 Do you have any friends who are of a different age group or race from you? What are some of the advantages of developing cross-generational and cross-cultural relationships?

🌀 Banneker's passion for his work motivated him when he faced various challenges. What are you most passionate about or driven by?

Right of Way: Patience

Despite his fulfilling work in laying out the capital, Benjamin Banneker's vision of publishing his almanac consumed him. New and extensive calculations were required for each year, and he wanted the almanac to be finished as quickly as possible, so each day that ticked by was crucial. After three months of intense work on the capital survey, the white-haired man rushed home and refocused his efforts on producing the almanac. He worked tirelessly on the content, and he patiently contacted publisher after publisher until one finally agreed to print the almanac, which was first offered to the public in 1792.

The year before the almanac was published, Benjamin sent a handwritten copy of it to Thomas Jefferson (then secretary of state). In his letter to Jefferson, he explained: "I direct to you, as a present, a copy of an almanac which I have calculated for the succeeding [coming] year. . . . Although you may have the opportunity of perusing it after its publication, yet I choose to send it to you in manuscript previous thereto, that thereby you might not only have an earlier inspection but that you might also view it in my own handwriting." Jefferson was a noted scientist, and Banneker knew Jefferson would be interested in the mathematical and astronomical calculations.

He had another reason for sending his calculations to Jefferson, however: to prove the equality of the races. (Unfortunately, it was long argued by proslavery racists that the intellect of slaves was inferior to that of whites.) Banneker knew that Jefferson wanted slavery ended, for it had been Jefferson himself who had introduced in Congress the first proposal to ban slavery in America. Banneker believed that Jefferson could be an ally, so he acknowledged to the president: "Sir, I hope I may safely admit, in consequence of that report which hath reached me, . . . that you are measurably friendly and well disposed towards us . . . and that your sentiments are concurrent with mine, which are: that one universal Father hath given being to us

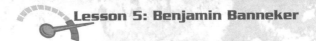

all and that He hath not only made us all of one flesh but that He hath also, without partiality, afforded us all the same sensations and endowed us all with the same faculties and that . . . we are all of the same family, and stand in the same relation to Him."

Jefferson was indeed impressed by Banneker and his work. He promptly wrote Banneker, praising him for the almanac and informing Benjamin that he had sent it on to scholars in France to be used as a tool in the fight for African-American equality. As Jefferson told Banneker, "I have taken the liberty of sending your Almanac to Monsieur de Condozett, Secretary of the Academy of Sciences at Paris and Member of the Philanthropic Society, because I considered it as a document to which your whole color had a right for their justification against the doubts which have been entertained of them. I am with great esteem, sir, your most obedient humble servant, Thomas Jefferson."

President Jefferson, when he sent Banneker's work to France, told the scholars, "I am happy to be able to inform you that we have now in the United States a Negro, the son of a black man born in Africa and of a black woman born in the United States, who is a very respectable mathematician. . . . He made me an almanac for the next year, which he sent me in his own handwriting and which I enclose to you. I have seen very elegant solutions of geometrical problems by him. Add to this that he is a very worthy and respectable member of society. He is a free man. I shall be delighted to see these instances of moral eminence so multiplied as to prove that [there is not] any difference in the structure of the parts on which intellect depends." Thomas Jefferson helped spread Banneker's notoriety across the globe, providing ammunition in the fight for African-American equality. Unfortunately, this fight wasn't brought to the limelight until many years later, and Banneker did not live to see much of the progress.

The year following Banneker's exchange of letters with Jefferson, the almanac was finally published (members of the antislavery society had learned about Banneker and helped him find a

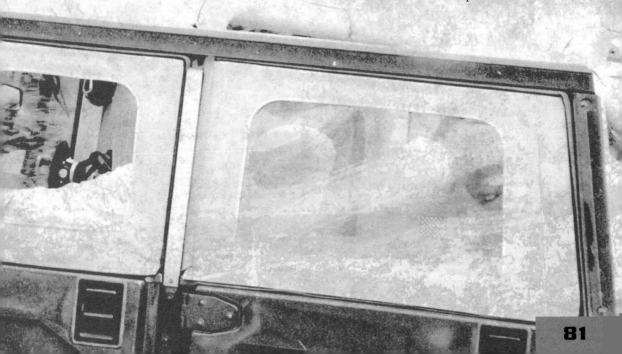

publisher for his almanac). That edition contained a written endorsement by Constitution signer James McHenry, founder of the Maryland Bible Society. While Banneker appreciated the help of the antislavery leaders, he also wanted his work recognized because of his scientific achievements, not just because he was an African-American scientist. As Banneker pondered this dilemma, he finally concluded that his competence as a mathematician and astronomer was not diminished by his involvement in the antislavery cause.

Benjamin Banneker's 1792 almanac was a best seller. So he patiently calculated measurements for other almanacs. His 1793 almanac continued as a best seller, and it not only included scientific tables with the time of every sunrise and sunset but also the correspondence between Banneker and Jefferson—and the proposed peace plan of Declaration signer Benjamin Rush.

"It is the indispensable duty of those, who maintain for themselves the rights of human nature, and who possess the obligations of Christianity, to extend their power and influence to the relief of every part of the human race."
Benjamin Banneker

Banneker's success did not alter his modest, gentlemanly manners, but it did allow him to devote his last years to the profession he loved. When stars sprinkled the night sky, Benjamin Banneker wrapped himself in a warm cloak, stretched out on the ground, and drank in the beauty of the heavens above. It is said that the only mathematical calculation he ever missed was the timing of his own death: He lived even longer than he had predicted, but as a Christian he would have understood that his days were really in God's hands and that only God knew when his life would end.

Choose one of the following projects:

1. **Create Your Own Almanac**
   Collect information similar to what Benjamin Banneker kept for his almanac (high and low temperatures, time of sunrise and sunset, moon phases, weather, precipitation, etc.). Keep track of your findings for one week and record them. (If you'd like to find out other types of information that appear in almanacs, you can find a copy of an almanac at the library or go to www.almanac.com or www.farmersalmanac.com.)

2. **Equal Rights Time Line**
   Benjamin Banneker didn't live to see many of the advancements made in the antislavery or equal rights movements. Create a time line of at least ten significant milestones for African-American rights. Include the year and a summary of each event, as well as where Banneker fit into the chronology.

3. **Stargazing**
   Print out a constellation chart that gives the names and locations of various stars. Take it outside with you on a clear night and see how many constellations you can identify. Then come up with some way to reflect on your stargazing experience, such as writing a journal entry, painting a picture, composing song lyrics, or writing a poem.

Stop and Ponder (for Group Discussion)

Benjamin Banneker spent large amounts of time in solitude, stretched out on the ground and drinking in the beauty of the heavens above. The many busy activities and regular noise of our everyday lives today often rob us of opportunities for solitude. Have you considered the possibility that patiently spending time in quiet contemplation might add depth of meaning to your life?

You're in the Driver's Seat
Setting Goals

Benjamin Banneker wanted to publish an almanac. He pursued his dream with patience and influenced others to help him achieve his goal. Banneker defined his vision, worked hard on it for many years, and produced a useful product. In time, his dream became a reality.

Have you wanted something so much that you couldn't even sleep? You tossed and turned and dreamed of achieving your goal, but you weren't quite sure how to make your dream a reality. The following steps will help guide you in the right direction.

1. Find a quiet place of solitude. Leave ringing cell phones and blaring music and friends behind for now.
2. Carve out a period of time (at least thirty minutes) for you to be alone and think. If possible, go to a park or your backyard and listen to the sounds in nature, but don't talk to anyone. For the first ten minutes, sit quietly and simply relax.
3. As you think about the following, record your thoughts in a journal:

● **Daydream about goals you hope to accomplish**
> today
> this week
> this month
> this year

● **Consider who might be able to help you achieve these goals. How do the goals of your family members and friends impact your vision? Beside each of your goals, write down the names of people who could help you achieve that goal.**

● **Decide what character traits you will need in order to be successful in meeting your goals. Make a list**

and circle the three traits that seem most important (or that you think need most work), and commit to focusing on one each week.

Worldview
Biology: How did life originate, and what difference does it make?

Benjamin Banneker considered science and religion compatible. His letter to Thomas Jefferson leaves no doubt that he believed in a Creator; he wrote, "one universal Father hath given being to us all. . . ." So his answer to the origin of life is clear—Benjamin Banneker believed that life began with God.

Numerous prominent and accomplished scientists through the ages—those responsible for some of the greatest discoveries—believed in God, including Isaac Newton, Robert Boyle, Johannes Kepler, Wernher von Braun, and so many others. They did not see a conflict between science and the God of the Bible.

Map Your Way
"The heavens declare the glory of God; the skies proclaim the work of his hands."
Psalm 19:1

Your viewpoint on the origin of life matters. Before you proceed on your life's journey, think about these questions:

● **How did life originate? What difference does it make?**

● **Is it possible for belief in God and scientific study to coexist? Explain your answer.**

DVD Reflection

Watch the DVD segment for Lesson 5 and complete the following activities:

Benjamin Banneker
Man of Science

Three ways Benjamin Banneker learned:

Three innovations of Banneker:

Three obstacles Banneker overcame:

Sudoku Puzzle

Benjamin Banneker loved numbers and logic. If Sudoku puzzles had been popular in his day, he probably would have been a master.

Directions: Complete the grid so that every row, column, and 3 x 3 box contains every digit from 1 to 9. (You can go to http://en.wikipedia.org/wiki/Sudoku or www.dailysudoku.co.uk/sudoku/index.shtml to learn more about Sudoku and other math puzzles and to solve a daily Sudoku puzzle.)

5	3	4	6	7	8	9	1	2
6	7	2	1	9	5	3	4	8
1	9	8	3	4	2	5	6	7
8	5	9	7	6	1	4	2	3
4	2	6	8	5	3	7	9	1
7	1	3	9	2	4	8	5	6
9	6	1	5	3	7	2	8	4
2	8	7	4	1	9	6	3	5
3	4	5	2	8	6	1	7	9

For Further Study

Geography
Federal Territory
Washington DC
Maryland
Patapsco River

Historical Context
Antislavery movement
Maryland Bible Society
Civil War
Civil rights movement

Significant Individuals and Groups
Molly Walsh
Quakers
George Ellicott
Andrew Ellicott
Thomas Jefferson
James McHenry

Terms
surveyor
indentured servant
bullock
drafting
drop-leaf table
ephemeris

Additional Resources
Silvio A. Bedini, *The Life of Benjamin Banneker* (Baltimore: Maryland Historical Society, 1984). This definitive biography of Benjamin Banneker records his unusual achievements and the impact of his intellectual accomplishments as an African-American man of science in the eighteenth century.

Lesson 6

NCSS Curriculum Standards

IV. Individual Development and Identity

Why do people behave as they do?

VII. Production, Distribution, and Consumption

How are goods and services to be distributed?

VI. Power, Authority, and Governance

How do nations respond to conflict?

Performance Expectations

Students will be able to:

1. Evaluate the impact of acts of altruism and other behaviors on individuals and groups.

2. Explain and illustrate how values and beliefs influence different economic decisions.

3. Apply economic concepts and reasoning when evaluating historical and contemporary social developments and issues.

4. Describe the ways nations and organizations respond to forces of unity and diversity affecting order and security.

LESSON 6:
Haym Salomon

Questions to Ask Yourself throughout This Unit

- Why would a Polish immigrant forfeit his own fortune for the Revolutionary War?

- What beliefs motivated Haym Salomon to make sacrifices for the cause of freedom?

- What economic and ethical principles can students learn from the life of Haym Salomon?

Fasten Your Seat Belt

Haym Salomon was an American Patriot during the American Revolution. His financial genius helped keep the Continental Army afloat during some of the most crucial days of the Revolutionary War, providing Washington's troops with critical supplies during the closing chapters of the war. It is unlikely that the Americans could have won the Battle of Yorktown to end the Revolution without the help of the French. Salomon made this success possible when he helped raise money to bring French troops and the French fleet to the United States. He also served as a spy for the United States. In addition to risking his life for his country, he provided at least $200,000 of his own money (almost $3.5 million by today's standards) to the Revolutionary cause.

Rebecca Machado Phillips, a prominent Jewish woman in colonial America, was the director of the Female Benevolent Society, one of the first Jewish charities in America.

Salomon, an American Jewish Patriot originally from Poland, was one of many from foreign lands who came to America and who fought for American liberty. For example, American Revolutionary generals Casimir Pulaski and Tadeusz Kosciuszko were also of Polish descent. (Pulaski headed the American soldiers on horseback and has been called "the father of the American cavalry." Kosciuszko, as chief engineer for the Continental Army, built fortified defenses and a number of important American military forts.) In addition to Salomon, there were several other American Jews who were part of the American Revolution: Francis Salvador (the first Jew to give his life for America), Abraham Levy and Phillip Russell (brave soldiers who endured the devastating winter at Valley Forge), and Mordecai Sheftell (a Patriot leader who was twice captured and made a prisoner of war by the British).

A Look in the Rearview Mirror
The Torch of Liberty

Before Haym Salomon landed on the shores of America, a fire burned deep within him. In Europe he had experienced the persecution that Russians had targeted against those who lived in Poland. As a Jew, he knew the harshness of religious oppression that for centuries had wounded his Jewish people, who so often had been the objects of religious persecution in Europe. When the young immigrant set foot in America in 1772, a yearning flared within him, springing from the depths of his soul—a passion for liberty, both civil and religious.

Haym Salomon arrived in New York City during turbulent times. Tension was building between America and her mother country, Great Britain. A desire for freedom dominated the hearts of many Americans, especially the Sons of Liberty, and there was a growing resistance to British tyranny. The tension was originally caused by the 1765 Stamp Act. Passed by the British Parliament, it had been like striking a match in a powder keg. The Sons of Liberty saw the Stamp Act as a clear violation of the British Bill of Rights—a violation of "no taxation without representation." They therefore organized a boycott of English goods, resulting in the Boston Tea Party and other acts of protest.

Rebecca Gratz was a devout Jew who helped establish and manage humanitarian and educational institutions for women and children. She is believed to be the model for Rebecca of York, the heroine of Ivanhoe, *by Sir Walter Scott.*

The British response to the Americans' desire for justice and liberty was harsher and more tyrannical rule. Both the civil and religious liberties of Americans were threatened. The British even sent troops against the Americans—and then demanded that the colonists pay for the troops that were oppressing them! The Patriots again resisted, and the inferno flared, with leaders such as Patrick Henry expressing the sentiments of many when he proclaimed, "Give me liberty or give me death!"

When Salomon arrived in New York City, he found a home on Wall Street—a narrow and ancient street that ran beside the New York Harbor. (It was called Wall Street because in the 1600s, the early Dutch settlers of New York City had built a wall along the harbor to protect themselves from Native Americans and pirates. A pathway developed along that wall that grew into a street, which was later called Wall Street. In 1792 a number of financial leaders with businesses on Wall Street agreed to work together to sell and trade financial securities, thus birthing the economic activity that makes Wall Street famous today.) In 1776, only four years after Haym had arrived in the colonies, the Americans declared independence from Great Britain. The British responded by attacking New York. One of the early battles was the Battle of Long Island, just outside New York City. In that battle, British commander General Howe defeated and drove off the American forces; he then entered unprotected New York City and occupied it for the next seven years, until the end of the Revolution.

In the midst of that occupation, Salomon was surrounded by British enemies, but he faithfully served the Patriot cause, quietly gathering information and supplying it to the Continental Army until the British arrested him and threw him into prison on September 22, 1776. Becoming a British prisoner of war was often a fatal experience for Americans—especially when they were placed in the New York prisoner-of-war camps. (In the American Revolution, more Americans lost their lives in British prisons than were killed on the battlefield by British bullets.) Salomon was imprisoned in Sugar House Prison—a brick sugar warehouse that the British had converted into a prison. The prisoners there were often starved, and since the prison had no roof, prisoners frequently became sick from exposure to the cold rain or biting snow. The death toll at Sugar House was

extremely high, and the prison earned its grim reputation with good reason.

Salomon's health suffered greatly while in prison, but eventually, because he spoke fluent German (as well as French, Polish, Russian, and Italian), he received better treatment. The British had hired seventeen thousand Hessians to fight against the Americans. (The Hessians were German soldiers recruited to fight on the side of the British, and they committed many atrocities against the Americans.) Most of the Hessians could not speak a word of English, so when the British discovered that Haym spoke fluent German, they made him an interpreter and moved him to a better location. He translated their orders to the prisoners, but he also began telling the Hessians about opportunities in America and convinced many to desert the British army. Salomon used his new position to help other prisoners as well—and to continue spying on the British.

Salomon was eventually released from Sugar House. He returned to his business and married Rachel Franks, who soon gave birth to a baby boy. Haym secretly continued to help the Americans and even sheltered wounded Patriots in his home. One night his Loyalist (pro-British) neighbors heard the moans of a wounded American soldier and reported Salomon to the authorities. He was again arrested; this time he was officially declared a spy and sentenced to be hanged at sunrise on August 11, 1778.

Even though known spies such as Salomon were guarded especially closely so they could not communicate with anyone, the Sons of Liberty learned of Salomon's plight. They smuggled a message to him and planned an escape route. Salomon managed to conceal a string of gold coins, purchase his freedom, and escape into the black night, following the planned escape route until he arrived safely among the American military forces at Dobbs Ferry, just north of New York City. Leaving behind his wife and one-month-old son (he felt confident that the British would not harm them), Haym headed to Philadelphia, where he set up a new business and was able to openly hold high the torch of liberty.

While Haym Salomon was one of many Founding Fathers from Poland who fought for America, there also were American Patriots from a number of other countries: the Marquis de Lafayette and Count d'Estaing from France (who provided America with both French troops and the French navy); Luis de Unzaga and Bernardo de Gálvez of Spain (who provided both military and financial aid to America); and Baron von Steuben of Germany (who forged the Continental Army into a disciplined, effective fighting force). America was established by people from many nations, faiths, and races who had a common love for God and for civil and religious liberty. In fact, even though most of the Founding Fathers were Christians, they provided religious liberty for all others. As Founding Father and Supreme Court justice Joseph Story explained, "The Catholic and the Protestant, the Calvinist and the Arminian, the Jew and the Infidel, may sit down at the common table of the national councils without any inquisition into their faith or mode of worship."

While the Founders of the United States provided religious liberty for all, many of them found particular common ground with Jews. Dr. Benjamin Rush (a Christian who was instrumental in the Sunday school movement in America, founded America's first Bible society, and signed the Declaration of Independence) watched a federal parade in Philadelphia and noted, "The rabbi of the Jews locked in the arms of two ministers of the Gospel was a most delightful sight. There could not have been a more happy emblem."

John Adams, another Christian signer of the Declaration, declared, "I will insist that the Hebrews have done more to civilize men than any other nation. . . . [They] preserve and propagate to all mankind the doctrine of a supreme, intelligent, wise, almighty Sovereign of the Universe, which I believe to be the great essential principle of all morality, and consequently of all civilization."

Other prominent Christian Founding Fathers—including George Washington, John Winthrop, and Elias Boudinot— held a similar respect for the Jews. This is why, historically speaking, America is described as having a Judeo-Christian heritage; from this heritage flows religious liberty for others. Haym Salomon was one of the Jewish Founders who helped provide both civil and religious freedom in America.

1. What early experiences fueled Salomon's pursuit of liberty?

The religious persecution and restrictions on freedom Salomon saw in Poland during his early years impacted the young man.

2. Why do you think Salomon placed such a high priority on establishing a society that protected religious liberty?

Salomon and the other Founding Fathers had witnessed persecution in other countries, and they did not want American citizens to experience similar restrictions. They wanted to build a new nation that would be characterized by both civil and religious freedom, recognizing that if people are not free to worship, they are not really free.

3. Why was Salomon willing to risk his life for his new country?
His love of liberty was greater than his desire to protect his own life.

School Zone Ahead
Winning on Wall Street [Math and Technology Activity]

The British diligently tried to keep supplies from reaching the Patriots in America by using their navy to set up blockades around American ports such as New York City, Philadelphia, and Charleston. Despite these blockades, courageous seamen found ways to elude the British ships and enter the ports, and whenever a ship broke through and docked in Philadelphia, Salomon was a middleman in the exchange of goods. He would purchase cargo (such as flour) for the market value of five dollars a barrel; he would then sell that flour in places such as Havana, Cuba, where it might go for as much as twenty dollars per barrel. His profits on such transactions were substantial, but so were the risks. That is, the flour for which he had paid five dollars a barrel might be captured by the British on its way to Cuba—or the ship could be destroyed by storms. In such cases, Haym would lose everything he had invested in that load of cargo. Today, speculators can trade in the futures market with the opportunity to make large profits, but just as in the time of Haym Salomon, playing the market also involves great risk.

1. Research various stocks, tracking historical trends and the stocks' current status. You can check stocks using the newspaper or the Internet (www.nasdaq.com; www.dowjones.com).

You can also register your class for a stock market simulation at a site such as www.smg2000.org or www. nationalsms.com for a minimal fee.

2. You will be allocated an imaginary sum of money, such as $5,000.

On a set day, you can purchase stocks and begin building your imaginary portfolio.

3. Graph stock movements over a designated time period. You may sell individual stocks and purchase other stocks during the project.

Historical Marker
The Price of Freedom

On the morning of November 3, 1781, overjoyed Philadelphians gathered along the streets to watch a celebration parade. Two dozen soldiers marched through the city, displaying the captured British colors taken by General George Washington and his troops when they defeated the British at Yorktown. The American and French flags led the way, waving triumphantly at the front of the parade. Haym, watching from his office on Front Street, rejoiced as the pageant passed. The procession finally ended when the captured colors were placed before the Continental Congress at Independence Hall.

Following the parade, Robert Morris, a signer of the Declaration of Independence and a financial leader in Congress, contacted Haym Salomon to discuss an idea. Even though the Continental Army had grabbed military victory from the British in the largest and most important battle of the Revolution, the crisis was far from over. (In fact, it would be two years after the victory at Yorktown before the British would officially acknowledge the end of the Revolution.) As winter loomed, General Washington and General Rochambeau (the leader of the French forces that were fighting alongside the Americans) wanted to attack New York and take it back from the British, but the American army was bankrupt—the American troops were starving, wearing rags, and demanding long-overdue wages (some had gone three years without being paid).

General Washington recognized the financial needs of the army, as well as the financial expertise of Robert Morris. So in 1781, Morris was appointed by Congress as the national superintendent of finance. Morris had already raised much money to fund the American Revolution, using both his shrewd business practices and his personal wealth to equip the army for fighting the British. However, the difficulties at the end of the war seemed insurmountable: The new government had no treasury, no tax system, and no central national governing power—not to mention the fact that there were thirteen individual states often jealously competing with each other and disagreeing over policy.

Therefore, despite the recent and brilliant battlefield victories—including the one at Yorktown—the entire Revolutionary cause stood on the brink of disaster due to lack of funds. Morris sought to avoid financial collapse and designed a plan for the struggling government, but the success of his plan depended on obtaining assistance from one of the best financial minds in Philadelphia: Haym Salomon.

Penina Moise was the first female Jewish poet and hymn writer in America. Despite the cultural limitations for Jewish women—and women in general—during her day, Moise's writings left a mark on history, and her hymns are still sung in Reform congregations today.

After escaping from the British in New York City in 1778, Salomon arrived in Philadelphia without a dime. Yet even though he had no money, he still had his brain. And with his understanding of foreign markets and remarkable knowledge of finance and commerce, he launched into business, dealing with bills of exchange and securities. He experienced phenomenal financial success and quickly earned a fortune—through honest means, hard work, and sharp wit. He was a successful businessman who was also wholly devoted to the Revolutionary cause. Morris knew he could depend on Salomon. They met together frequently, and both men worked feverishly to save the government from bankruptcy.

The financial difficulties they faced at that time would be almost unimaginable for us today. For example, during the Revolution, each of the thirteen colonies had its own money and coins. (Imagine—thirteen different sets of currency! Just going from North Carolina to South Carolina would have required exchanging money!) Morris realized that the country needed a central bank, so on January 7, 1782, the National Bank of North America opened for business. Haym and several of his Jewish friends bought shares in the first subscription, for the Jewish community in America wholly supported the Patriot cause. (In fact, out of two hundred Jewish families in Philadelphia, only one sided with the British.) Searching tirelessly for money for the government, Salomon called on his many friends, and because of his impeccable honesty and unquestionable patriotism, he charged practically nothing for his services. Whenever the government coffers were empty, Salomon faithfully responded to Morris's call for help. Haym was so competent and trustworthy in his financial activities that even the foreign governments assisting America relied on him. The French appointed Salomon paymaster general of the French forces in America. In addition, he helped process the loans that France, Holland, and Spain made to America.

When the National Bank opened in 1782, it helped the Revolutionary cause, but it was not enough. Government employees and soldiers bombarded the bank with demands for back pay, but the military still needed money to operate. Since the bank was unable to supply all the requests, Salomon extended his personal funds to help notable leaders such as James Madison, Baron von Steuben, James Wilson, Alexander

Hamilton, and Edmund Randolph—as well as others too numerous to mention. James Madison, for example, acknowledged, "I have for some time . . . been a pensioner [dependent] on the favor of Haym Salomon." Morris and Salomon painstakingly sought funds to deal with each new financial crisis, and each of them repeatedly gave from his personal resources in response to the unending calls for help. Eventually the constant stress ruined the finances and the health of both men.

Haym Salomon sacrificed his own fortune and talents for the cause of liberty. His patriotic service helped ensure that a starry red, white, and blue flag of victory (instead of a white flag of surrender) fluttered over the new nation.

Choose one of the following activities:

1. Bank Flowchart

Haym Salomon was a key player in the creation of the first national bank. Make a flowchart that portrays how a modern bank works. Include the percentages for money that is deposited, put in reserve, and loaned out. (You may want to check an encyclopedia or http://money.howstuffworks.com/bank.htm to find this information.)

2. Checking Account Simulation

Create a mock checking account. Using sample forms from a local bank or off the Internet, make deposits and withdrawals, write and endorse checks, and reconcile your account.

3. Military Funding Graph

Haym Salomon's financial contributions were vital to the success of the Continental Army. The method of acquiring military funds has changed dramatically since the Revolutionary War, however. The current defense budget in the United States is approximately $300 billion and no longer comes from the pockets of individual donors. Do some research about wartime expenses during the Revolutionary War, and make a pie chart designating the various military expenses.

Right of Way: Generosity

Haym Salomon understood economics and he made, lost, and remade a fortune. But beyond his financial skills, several important character traits were apparent in his life. First, he earned and used his fortune honestly; a study of his life illuminates a lifetime of upright business dealings. Next, he was a man of fidelity; he could be trusted completely. He was also a man of integrity; nations, as well as individuals, knew that he was a man of his word. And Salomon was generous; he was willing to use his money and his financial expertise for the good of others. In addition to helping many prominent statesmen, Salomon loaned money to congressmen and military officers in need. He did not count on them to be able to repay their loans—

and the interest and commissions he charged were well below market rates.

All these character traits are taught in the Scriptures of the Jewish faith, and Haym Salomon learned those lessons well and exemplified in his own life what he had been taught from those principles. (In fact, Salomon contributed frequently to his synagogue and donated a fourth of the funds required for their new building.) Haym's personal generosity—as well as his ability to motivate others to give to the American cause—was essential to the success of the Continental Army and the establishment of America as an independent nation.

Haym Salomon and Robert Morris earned hundreds of thousands of dollars during the last decade of the eighteenth century, yet they both died in debt and left their families bankrupt. They sacrificed their time, abilities, and finances for the cause of freedom. Regrettably, the United States government refused to reimburse Salomon's family for the funds he loaned during the Revolutionary War, even though congressional

committees recommended that the claims be paid. Nevertheless, so great was Salomon's contribution to American independence that the United States Postal Service issued a stamp hailing Salomon as the "financial hero of the American Revolution."

In 1941 a monument in honor of Haym Salomon, Robert Morris, and George Washington was dedicated in Chicago. General George Washington stands larger than life at the center of the sculpture, holding the hands of Haym Salomon and Robert Morris. Words spoken by President George Washington are carved at the base of the monument: "The Government of the United States, which gives bigotry [discrimination] no sanction [approval], to persecution no assistance, requires only that they who live under its protection should demean themselves as good citizens in giving it on all occasions their effectual support." The monument symbolizes the spirit of American unity. At the dedication, the mayor of Chicago said, "George Washington and his friend, Robert Morris, were Christians; Haym Salomon was a Jew. . . . These three, though of

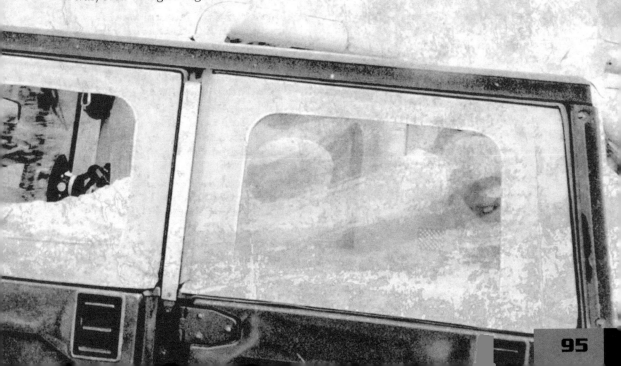

widely different walks of life, labored together in a common cause in order that the American way of life . . . might be guaranteed to future generations. . . . President Franklin Roosevelt called the three Revolutionary leaders 'the great triumvirate of patriots.'"

1. **Name two abilities that helped Salomon in his role as "financial hero of the American Revolution."**

Salomon understood economics; his financial brilliance and work experience in Europe helped him develop a thorough understanding of international finance. His wide travels and fluency in languages helped him establish important financial connections he willingly used for the Patriot cause. He had the ability to quickly accumulate wealth, much of which he donated to the Continental Army.

2. **List two character traits that marked Salomon's interactions with individuals from other countries, as well as his fellow Patriots. Give an example that illustrates each trait.**

Students may want to address Salomon's honesty, integrity, generosity, mediation skills, or loyalty.

3. **What beliefs motivated Haym Salomon to make sacrifices for the cause of freedom?**

Salomon's love of liberty and his commitment to the principles in Jewish Scripture influenced his behavior. His religious foundation provided a basis for moral and upright actions.

Stop and Ponder (for Group Discussion)

● Describe someone you know who gives generously—of his or her money, skills, or time.

● Do you think having wealth is dangerous or advantageous? Explain.

You're in the Driver's Seat
Serving Others

Some students in the stock market activity made profits. Others lost money. Occasionally success is the result of luck, but more often it comes from diligence—from hard work and clear thinking—for *every* individual has unique abilities and interests that can be used to bring success in some area.

Your teacher will divide the class into groups. Each group will:

1. **Brainstorm a list of difficulties that people in the world face—in your area and globally.**

2. **Do research to find organizations that assist people who are dealing with these issues.**

3. **Narrow your list and vote on one organization you'd like to support.**

4. **Decide on a fund-raiser your group can do together, and create a detailed plan for it.**

5. **Implement your fund-raiser, and donate the funds to the organization you selected.**

6. **Evaluate your project's success.**

Worldview
Economics: What Are the Principles for Making and Spending Money Wisely?

Haym Salomon understood economics, both in terms of business principles and ethical principles. The following summaries reflect his philosophy on money:

1. Know your business.
2. Work hard.
3. Make money honestly.
4. Respect people's rights.
5. Stick to your principles.
6. Give generously.

What economic principles do *you* live by?

Map Your Way

"A good name is more desirable than great riches; to be esteemed is better than silver or gold. . . . A generous man will himself be blessed, for he shares his food with the poor."
Proverbs 22:1, 9

Before you rev up your engine and speed down the road, read the proverb above and think about the following questions:

● **How do you handle money?**

● **How does your use of money reflect your worldview?**

DVD Reflection

Watch the DVD segment for Lesson 6 and complete the following activities:

Haym Salomon
Financial Hero of the Revolution

Dave Stotts mentions that it is highly unlikely America could have won the Revolutionary War without the help of the French. People from many European countries were engaged in the Revolutionary War. List European countries mentioned in this DVD segment.

Salomon was a first-generation American. How many generations has your family lived in America? From what country (or countries) did your ancestors come to the United States?

One thing I could learn from Haym Salomon about spending my money:

For Further Study

Geography
Poland
New York City, New York
Dobbs Ferry, New York
Philadelphia, Pennsylvania
Yorktown, New York

Historical Context
Polish-Russian relations in
  the seventeenth and
  eighteenth centuries
Jewish persecution in
  eighteenth century Europe
Holocaust
Stamp Act (1765)
British Bill of Rights
Boston Tea Party
New York Stock Exchange
Battle of Long Island
Battle of Yorktown
National Bank of North America

Significant Individuals and Groups
Sons of Liberty
Casimir Pulaski
Tadeusz Kosciuszko
Francis Salvador
Abraham Levy
Phillip Russell
Mordecai Sheftell
Patrick Henry
General William Howe
Hessians
Loyalists
Marquis de Lafayette
Count d'Estaing
Luis de Unzaga
Bernardo de Galvez

Baron von Steuben
Joseph Story
John Winthrop
Elias Boudinot
Robert Morris
General Rochambeau

Terms
cavalry
tyranny
boycott
futures market
superintendent of finance
bills of exchange
securities
subscriptions
coffers
paymaster general

Additional Resources
Charles Edward Russell, *Haym Salomon and the Revolution* (New York: Cosmopolitan Book Co., 1930). This biography of Haym Salomon tells the life story of a great American Patriot whose financial genius and generosity earned him the title "financial hero of the American Revolution."

C. Keith Wilbur, *Revolutionary Soldier: 1775–1783* (Guilford, Conn.: Globe Pequot, 1993). This book offers illustrations of many areas of Revolutionary military life, including weapons, uniforms, medicine, food, and shelter.

Lesson 7

NCSS Curriculum Standards

I. Culture

How do belief systems, such as religion or political ideals, influence culture?

II. Time, Continuity, and Change

What happened in the past, and how am I connected to those in the past?

IV. Individual Development and Identity

Why do people behave as they do? What influences how people learn, perceive, and grow?

VI. Power, Authority, and Governance

How can individual rights be protected within the context of majority rule?

X. Civic Ideals and Practices

What is civic participation, and how can I be involved?

Performance Expectations

Students will be able to:

1. Explain how information and experiences may be interpreted by people from diverse cultural perspectives and frames of reference.

2. Develop critical sensitivities such as empathy and skepticism regarding attitudes, values, and behaviors of people in different historical contexts.

3. Describe the ways family, religion, gender, and nationality contribute to the development of a sense of self.

4. Examine persistent issues involving the rights, roles, and status of the individual in relation to the general welfare.

5. Analyze the effectiveness of selected citizen behaviors in realizing the stated ideals of a democratic republican form of government.

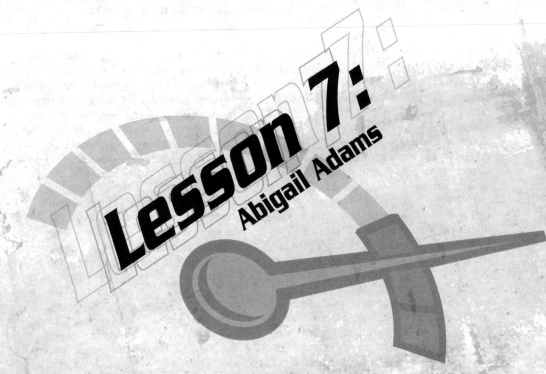

Lesson 7:
Abigail Adams

Questions to Ask Yourself throughout This Unit

- How did Abigail Adams's thirst for knowledge open doors of learning normally closed to women?

- What lessons can both men and women learn from Abigail Adams?

- What character traits enabled Abigail Adams to become a woman of great influence?

Fasten Your Seat Belt

Have you ever felt the frustration of "If only . . ."? The pleas often sound something like this: "If only I were . . . taller, smarter, prettier, richer, thinner . . . my life would be so much better." In the 1740s, there might have been cause to say "If only . . ." merely from being born a girl. In Abigail Adams's lifetime, girls had limited opportunities; their lives were mapped out for them from childhood to old age. They received almost no formal education; the little schooling they did receive was just enough for them to manage household and domestic duties. Women of the Revolutionary era did not even have legal rights, including the right to vote.

Yet even though Abigail faced major disadvantages because she was a girl, she did not complain. Her father was a famous pastor, and as a devout Christian herself, she adhered to the command of Philippians 2:14: "Do everything without complaining or arguing." As another product of her faith, Abigail lived a life of virtue—striving to make morally excellent decisions. As she explained, "The only sure and permanent foundation of virtue is religion; and the foundation . . . is the belief of the one only God, as a Being infinitely wise, just, and good."

On many occasions in her life, Abigail—a smart, ambitious, and determined girl—could have screamed in frustration, "This is not fair! And it's not right! If only I had been born a boy!" But rather than pouting or complaining about her many disadvantages and the lack of opportunities she faced, Abigail made the most of her circumstances. She supported her famous husband, John Adams, during his long political career and was an indispensable help to him, becoming his closest adviser. Additionally, she served as a war correspondent for him during the Revolution, successfully managed a business and made investments, and raised a family whose positive impact on America lasted for generations. Not only was she the wife of one president (John Adams), but she was the mother of another (John Quincy Adams). Throughout her long life, she spoke out for the equality and freedom of all those who, like herself, had reason to feel "if only."

A Look in the Rearview Mirror
The Library

Whenever Elizabeth Smith couldn't find her daughter Abigail, she didn't have to look far; she knew where she would be.

After the cooking, cleaning, and sewing were done, Abigail would rush to her favorite room in the house: her father's library. Her father, Reverend William Smith, was a Congregational minister in Weymouth, Massachusetts, and he gave his children an unusual gift for the 1700s—full access to his extensive library—a rarity since books were scarce and expensive at that time. For girls, such a privilege was unheard of, but Reverend Smith's second daughter, Abigail, took full advantage of her father's generosity. Abigail passionately shared her father's love of books and the acquisition of knowledge. History records indicate that she read widely in poetry, drama, history, theology, and political theory. Through her father's books, Abigail learned about the world far beyond the boundaries of her small colonial town. She also developed a love for learning that she retained throughout her life, preparing her for an important role in American history.

Girls born in the late 1700s learned only reading and writing skills, along with a small bit of math. They were taught no more than what was needed to read the Bible, write letters, and manage household accounts. Subjects such as world history, politics, science, and literature simply weren't taught to girls in those days. But the Smith girls were fortunate. They had a father who loved God, providing them with the foundation for an unshakable faith that remained throughout life. He also wanted all his children—even his daughters—to share in his passion for learning and reading.

Even though her father gave her full use of his private library, Abigail never had the privilege of attending school. She was mostly self-taught, which left gaps in her education. Her spelling was poor, she did not know how to use punctuation properly, and her primitive penmanship always embarrassed her. Yet on her own, she managed to master reading in French and Latin. By the time she was an adult, Abigail Smith Adams was known as one of the best-read women of her time.

Abigail's parents had a significant impact on Abigail's childhood; another important influence was her Grandmother Quincy. Although Abigail was a shy child, she was also strong willed. Her mother hoped that time spent with Grandmother Quincy might help Abigail become more compliant. Grandmother Quincy, however, saw the situation differently: While she opposed the idea of being strong willed for selfish purposes, she advocated a strong will in standing for what is right. Abigail simply needed to be pointed in the right direction. Grandmother Quincy used to say, "Wild colts make the best horses," and she found Abigail's determined spirit refreshing. She was proud of her granddaughter's quick intelligence and never said a word about her being too bookish. Abigail adored her grandmother. Until the end of Abigail's life, she relied on and spoke highly of the example and advice of Grandmother Quincy.

Abigail's desire to educate herself was a brave stance for a female in her day. The goals of most eighteenth-century girls centered around marriage and family. A woman who was "too educated" feared that she'd be passed over by suitors in favor of more seemingly feminine and lighthearted women.

The first time John Adams met Abigail Smith, he was not particularly impressed. However, two years later, when the two met again, John began to appreciate Abigail's intellect and cleverness, describing her as "sensible and active." Reading created a bond between Abigail and John, who was a Harvard graduate trying to launch his career as a lawyer. During their courtship, John often brought Abigail books as gifts, which they read and discussed together. Starting with their second meeting and continuing throughout their fifty-four-year marriage, John, who addressed his wife as "Miss Adorable," relied heavily on Abigail's sharp intellectual advice and unwavering support.

Abigail never lost her childhood thirst for knowledge. Although she was a wife and the mother of five, in the late 1780s she had the opportunity to study science, a subject to which few women of that day were allowed access. She signed up for a series of twelve lectures and attended five: on electricity, magnetism, hydrostatics, optics, and pneumatics— advanced and newly developing subjects in that day. The experience inspired Abigail Adams and gave her insight into a vast new world of ideas. "It was like going into a beautiful country, which I never saw before," she wrote, "a country which our American females are not permitted to visit or inspect."

1. **Why was access to a library considered a special privilege for Abigail Smith?**

Books were cherished possessions to people living during the time period when Abigail lived. Many females did not have the opportunity to learn to read, let alone have access to a variety of books.

2. **Compare and contrast educational opportunities for American girls in the 1700s to educational opportunities for girls today.**

During the 1700s, education for girls differed considerably from education for boys. Girls' schooling was almost completely nonacademic, focusing on homemaking, social graces such as letter writing, and domestic skills. Girls did not receive the general academic education that boys received, which included math, writing, language, and reading. A few girls, like Abigail Smith, did not go to school but were given a solid education in the classics by their fathers. Today, for the most part, females have the same educational opportunities as males have. They attend the same schools, learn the same subjects, and have access to the same careers.

3. **Describe the influence of Abigail Adams's grandmother in Abigail's life.**

Abigail's grandmother supported her desire to learn and encouraged her throughout her lifetime. She saw Abigail's strong will as an advantage and helped her channel it appropriately, and she gave advice that Abigail followed throughout her life.

Stop and Ponder (for Group Discussion)

Do you have a grandparent or another older person who supports or influences you? If so, how?

Have you (or someone you know) ever experienced a time when you were prevented from doing something based on your gender, age, race, or some other factor?

Detour: Title IX

Two centuries after Abigail Adams's efforts for women's rights, changes were still being made by the legal system to promote equal opportunities. In 1972, the Title IX Educational Amendment was enacted in the United States stipulating that "no person shall, on the basis of sex, be excluded from participation in, be denied the benefits of, or be subjected to discrimination under any education program or activity receiving federal financial assistance." This law makes it illegal to treat students differently on the basis of gender.

Historical Marker
A Patriot

During the Revolutionary War, while the men fought for America's freedom in government courts or on battlefields, the women did their part as Patriots on the home front. They went to military camps to help the army, boycotted British goods, and even served as spies. They tended the sick and wounded, raised money for the war, and defended their homesteads. They managed to feed their families with meager rations, and some secretly served as soldiers. The generals on both sides of the war acknowledged the strength of America's female Patriots. George Washington wrote, "You ladies are in the number of the best Patriots America can boast," and British general Lord Cornwallis lamented, "We may destroy all the men in America, and we shall still have all we can do to defeat the women."

Outspoken, determined, and innovative, Abigail Adams perfectly filled the role of a brave Patriot. She loved America passionately and hated England with equal force. She wrote of her sense of patriotism, "Difficult as the day is, cruel as the war has been . . . I would not exchange my country for the wealth of the Indies, or be any other than an American."

Abigail Adams faced many of the difficulties of the American Revolution by herself. The British wanted to find her husband, John, and execute him for his role in leading the American Patriots. He served as a delegate to the Continental Congress, and because of his great abilities, he was dispatched by Congress as a diplomat to Europe. Consequently, between his Congressional duties and his overseas assignments, John and Abigail went three years without seeing each other.

With John away from home, all the responsibilities of the family fell to Abigail. Raised with servants and the niceties of an upper-class lifestyle, she

now had not only the usual domestic household duties but also John's tasks. She suddenly had to get her hands dirty with farming and keep a business running—all on her own. Yet she managed the family farm and business so well that neighbors later reported to her husband that they had never seen his homestead look so good. She learned to make investments by herself, hire and fire servants, and plant at the right time. She also educated the children herself, providing them both with academic and spiritual training.

Throughout that period, the Revolution raged around the family. As John Quincy Adams later recalled, "My mother with her children lived in unintermitted [continual] danger of being consumed . . . in a conflagration [blaze of fire]. . . . I saw with my own eyes those fires—and heard Britannia's [Britain's] thunders in the battle of Bunker's Hill—and witnessed the tears of my mother (and mingled with them my own) at the fall of Warren, a dear friend of my father and a beloved physician to me." Night and day, Abigail and her children faced constant danger, with the enemy in close proximity to the family home.

Abigail Adams not only cared for her own family but also took in many who were homeless due to the war. And there were times when her precious family heirlooms were sacrificed for the cause of American freedom. As John Quincy Adams later recalled, "The Minutemen from a hundred towns in the Province were marching. . . . Many of them called at my father's house. . . . There were, then, in my father's kitchen some dozen or two of pewter spoons; and I well recollect going into the kitchen and seeing some of the men engaged in running [melting] those spoons into bullets for the use of the troops! Do you wonder that a boy of seven years of age who witnessed this scene should be a patriot?"

Because of Abigail's quick intelligence and clear thinking, espionage became a part of her role in the Revolution. John relied on her letters for detailed, accurate information about events in New England, including British plans and troop movements. John shared this information with Congress and later praised his wife to a friend, proudly declaring, "She has clearer and fuller intelligence than I can get from a whole committee of gentlemen."

Abigail Adams's contributions were not limited to political and military areas; she was also involved in social causes. As a young girl, Abigail accompanied her mother, a minister's wife who often visited the sick and the poor. Her mother's outward expression of her religious beliefs as she offered help to the helpless made a deep impression on Abigail. She had also been taught about the wrongs of slavery and the equality of all individuals before God, so it is not surprising that she spoke out forcefully against slavery. In one letter she wrote, "I wish most sincerely there was not a slave in the province. It always appears a most iniquitous scheme to me—[to] fight . . . for what we are daily robbing and plundering from those who have as good a right to freedom as we have." She clearly expressed her belief that it was wrong to fight for freedom from the British while denying that same freedom to others in America.

"If particular care and attention is not paid to the Ladies, we are determined to foment [start] a Rebellion, and will not hold ourselves bound by any laws in which we have no voice or Representation."
Abigail Adams

Once the colonies became an independent nation, Abigail Adams challenged the new leaders to rethink their views of women. Writing of her feelings to her husband, John, Abigail said, "Whilst [While] you are proclaiming peace and good will to Men, Emancipating all Nations, you insist upon retaining absolute power over wives." One of Abigail's greatest frustrations was that she had not received the classic education afforded to the males of her time. Abigail understood that an educated woman could better perform her duties as a wife, mother, and household manager. In another letter to John, she wrote, "You need not be told how much female education is neglected, nor how fashionable it has been to ridicule female learning." Abigail openly expressed her hope that in the new Republic: "If we mean to have Heroes, Statesmen, and Philosophers, we should have learned women."

During her lifetime, Abigail Adams witnessed significant improvement in the treatment of slaves when several northern states abolished slavery and extended to former slaves the right to vote. She also witnessed an improvement in attitudes toward women, as some academic schools for women were started. However, she did not experience the joy of seeing slavery abolished in the entire nation nor did she see major changes in the national policies regarding women. Yet her son John Quincy Adams, sixth president of the United States, took up Abigail's cause and was instrumental in the abolition of slavery. Others followed her lead in various struggles for equal rights, gradually improving opportunities for all people, regardless of race or gender.

1. Compare and contrast roles of American men and women during the Revolutionary War. How have these roles changed throughout history?

In the Revolutionary era, both men and women made vital contributions, and both experienced the trials and triumphs of the struggle for independence. While men frequently fought on the battlefields and participated in conventions and congresses, women primarily held down the home front, often assuming new roles and maintaining the family businesses. While some actually participated in military service, other women served as spies, enforced the economic side of the Revolution by boycotting British goods, tended the sick and wounded, and raised money for the war. Today men and women both work in the halls of Congress and in the military.

2. List three ways Abigail Adams served her country and her family during the Revolutionary War.

Abigail observed the enemy and sent both political and military intelligence on to her husband, who then shared it with Congress. She opened her home to Americans who had been displaced by the war. While her husband, John, was away from home working on the Declaration of Independence or traveling to Europe on behalf of the colonies, Abigail Adams managed the family farm, raised their children, and offered political advice to her husband and other leaders. Like many other women, she made it possible for her husband to contribute to the war efforts, and the American Revolution could not have been won nor the new nation established without the integral assistance and strength of the women.

3. Abigail Adams advocated for justice for many groups of people. Briefly describe three ways she sought to improve the lives of the oppressed. What beliefs do you think formed the foundation for her efforts for social reform?

She visited the sick and offered them care. She opened her home to those who had been displaced by the war. She wrote letters and engaged in dialogue with influential leaders in support of equal rights for women and slaves. Her efforts for social reform were supported by her religious faith and her strong-willed nature to fight for what was right.

School Zone Ahead
Family Feast (Technology/Family and Consumer Science Activity)

Abigail Adams's dinner table served as a place for sharing food and conversation with family members and friends. As a result of the shortages they experienced during the war years, they typically ate plain but substantial servings of foods such as turkey, roast beef, mince pie, plum pudding, and cranberry tart. Recipes from families in early America are available in books and on the Internet. Using an Internet search engine, such as Yahoo or Google, find a colonial recipe and prepare a dish for a class potluck meal. Helpful key words to use in your search: recipes, colonial America, Revolutionary War era, and food. A number of recipe books are also available, such as *Colonial Cooking* by Susan Dosier and *Revolutionary Recipes* by Patricia Mitchell.

Right of Way: Influence
Remember the Ladies

Abigail Adams, First Lady of the second president of the United States, wrote hundreds of letters over the course of her life that chronicled the history of our young country's hard road to independence. Her letters were witty, her descriptions of war times were vivid, and her opposition to Britain's rule was fearless. These letters tell the important story of the women who did their part for the war while at home—defending their homesteads, struggling with wartime shortages, running farms and businesses with minimal help, and teaching children during the interruption of formal education.

Because of her embarrassment over her poor penmanship and bad grammar, Abigail Adams begged her husband to destroy her letters to him, but fortunately for future generations, John Adams ignored her pleas. Today the historical value of Abigail Adams's letters is priceless, because they provide details of the American Revolution and clues to the past. But long ago, America's Founding Fathers felt the influence of her letters as well.

During America's struggle to become a nation in the 1700s, women were limited in what they could do for the war. Letter writing, however, was one of the social graces that young girls were taught. Abigail Adams, who had been writing since she was a child, wrote letters as part of her war efforts. Her letters advised her son, who was posted in Europe. Her letters encouraged and informed her husband, who because of his government duties, was often away from home. Abigail became good friends with another outspoken woman, Mercy Otis Warren, and fortunately for us, they lived just far enough apart to make communicating by letter necessary. Abigail's and Mercy's letters have survived the centuries, and they provide us a heartfelt, uncensored (from one friend to another) account of the political attitudes of that day. Abigail Adams also wrote frank letters to shapers of the country, such as John Lovell, a Continental Congress delegate, and Thomas Jefferson, a signer of the Declaration of Independence.

"Great necessities call out great virtues."
Abigail Adams

For ten years, Abigail Adams was regularly separated from her husband, John, who was either on diplomatic missions in Europe or tending to national business at the Continental Congress in Philadelphia. The separation produced a stream of letters in which Abigail served as his trusted war correspondent and political adviser. She also kept him informed about their business and farm, which she successfully managed in his absence. Her regular correspondence with John, as well as her skill in managing household affairs, allowed him to focus on the nation without worrying about his home or family. One of the most quoted sayings of Abigail Adams was actually written in a letter to her husband in the spring of 1776, while he was posted in Philadelphia. The British evacuation of Boston on March 17 freed America's leaders to establish new laws concerning government; relations with foreign powers; slavery; and, of particular interest to Abigail Adams, the status of women. Abigail seized the opportunity to speak out against the unequal treatment of women. She wrote to her husband, "In the new Code of Laws . . . I desire you would remember the ladies, and be more generous and favorable to them than your ancestors." Although John Adams replied that her request caused him to laugh, he eventually took her advice and championed for the rights of women.

Abigail's son John Quincy Adams traveled with his father in Europe at the age of ten. As any mother would, Abigail worried about her young, impressionable son, and she wrote letters to him on matters of life and morality. Abigail wrote, "Great learning and superior abilities . . . will be of little value and small estimation, unless virtue, honor, truth and integrity are added to them. And remember that you are accountable to your Maker for all your words and actions." One letter from Abigail to John Quincy records some advice that parents have given throughout history, causing children to groan at hearing it: "Whatever you undertake aim to make yourself perfect in it, for if it is worth doing at all, it is worth doing well."

John Quincy Adams, who followed in his father's footsteps and became the sixth American president, continued his mother's habit of writing. He wrote books and poetry, and from early childhood to old age kept a daily journal. Today, due in large part to the influence of his mother, John Quincy Adams's extensive, detailed journals provide us with an invaluable account of American history.

1. "Dear Abby" Letter

Much of what we know about Abigail Adams is from the thousands of letters she sent to her family, her husband, and various political figures. In addition to personal updates, her letters often included accounts of political events and her views on social issues. In many ways, Abigail was a woman ahead of her time, and she was not able to see most of the changes she dreamed of during her lifetime. Write a letter to Abigail, informing her of the changes that have taken place in our country since her death in the areas of slavery, women's rights, and education.

2. Women's Rights Time Line

Create a time line of significant events in women's rights. Include important individuals, laws, and milestones that contributed to equal opportunities for women in the United States.

3. Revolutionary Play

Abigail's friend Mercy Otis Warren was also a staunch supporter of the Patriot cause. In 1772 she published a satirical play called *The Adulateur*, which was intended to criticize Britain and promote the Revolution. Write a script for a play of your own with a theme similar to Mercy Warren's.

Stop and Ponder (for Group Discussion)

● What do you think of Abigail Adams's admonition, "If it is worth doing at all, it is worth doing well"?

● What advice have you received from parents or other leaders in your life?

You're in the Driver's Seat
Influencing Others

Abigail and John Adams loved and respected one another, working side by side as partners for over half a century. They discussed ideas with each other, their children, many Patriots, and leaders in Europe. As a result, they exercised far-reaching influence that impacted many generations. One of the primary ways their legacy has endured is through the letters they both wrote.

Although today we have many more modes of communication, letter writing is still a way to influence others. Writing letters to elected officials or to newspapers gives citizens an opportunity to state opinions and lobby for change.

Identify an issue that you feel strongly about. Consider addressing a situation in which a person or group of people is being treated unfairly at home, at school, in the community, or worldwide. Write a letter to influence someone in a position of authority to act in the way you support. Or write a letter expressing your opinion and reasons to back up your stance, and send it to the local newspaper or to your school paper with the intent of persuading readers to your point of view.

"Learning is not attained by chance. It must be sought for with ardor and attended to with diligence."
Abigail Adams

Worldview

Psychology: What is the basic nature of humans?

When Abigail Adams told her son, "Remember that you are accountable to your Maker for all your words and actions," she revealed a basic belief that she (and most people of her generation) held. She believed that her children and all people were morally responsible for their actions. As a Christian, she understood that her children faced temptations to do wrong but that they could choose to obey God's commands and do what was right. She also recognized that when they made wrong choices, they suffered the consequences for their misbehavior. When she was informed that her exceptionally gifted oldest child displayed arrogance, she wrote him a letter filled with motherly advice. Abigail told John Quincy that with all the advantages and opportunities afforded him through books, travel, and spending time with world leaders, it would be "unpardonable" for him "to have been a blockhead."

Map Your Way

"No discipline seems pleasant at the time, but painful. Later on, however, it produces a harvest of righteousness and peace for those who have been trained by it."
Hebrews 12:11

You face choices every day. Some of the decisions you make are relatively inconsequential, such as what clothes to wear or what to eat for lunch. Other decisions have significant repercussions, and the route you take may impact your whole life.

Sometimes we experience painful consequences as a result of poor choices we've made. Other times we experience pain as a result of discipline (either self-discipline or discipline by a leader).

● **Think about a time you experienced pain after making an unwise decision.**

● **Think about a time you experienced pain as a result of discipline.**

● **How did you learn from each experience? How was the pain in each situation different?**

DVD Reflection

Watch the DVD segment for Lesson 7 and complete the following activities:

Abigail Adams
Woman of Influence

Dave Stotts says that Abigail Adams did her part on the home front during the Revolutionary War. As you watch the DVD segment, see how many of the following letters you can use in listing ways Abigail Adams helped the Patriot cause during the war years.

E

S

PATRIOT

I

INVESTOR

N

A

G

WAR CORRESPONDENT

Abigail Adams's Advice:
To John Quincy Adams:
"Don't be a blockhead."

To John Adams:
"Remember the ladies."

What advice would you give to the president of the United States?

For Further Study

Geography
Weymouth, Massachusetts
Philadelphia, Pennsylvania
Boston, Massachusetts

Historical Context
Women's rights
1972 Title IX Educational Amendment
Continental Congress
Battle of Bunker Hill
Antislavery movement

Significant Individuals and Groups
John Adams
John Quincy Adams
General Lord Cornwallis
Minutemen
Mercy Otis Warren
John Lovell
Thomas Jefferson
Phillis Wheatley
Narcissa Whitman
Timothy Dwight
Emma Willard
Charles Finney

Terms
hydrostatics
optics
pneumatics
homestead
diplomat
espionage

Additional Resources
David McCullough, *John Adams* (New York: Simon & Schuster, 2001). In this powerful biography of John Adams's life, McCullough describes not only John's adventures as a Patriot and president but also the significant role his wife, Abigail, played as they worked side by side on behalf of the Revolutionary cause.

Mercy Otis Warren, *History of the Rise, Progress, and Termination of the American Revolution* (Indianapolis: Liberty Classics, 1988). Mercy Otis Warren has been described as perhaps the most formidable female intellectual in eighteenth-century America. This work is an exciting and comprehensive study of the events of the American Revolution, from the Stamp Act Crisis through the ratification of the Constitution.

Harry Clinton Green and Mary Wolcott Green, *Wives of the Signers: The Women behind the Declaration of Independence* (Aledo, Tex.: WallBuilder Press, 1997). This book describes the women who, alongside their husbands, experienced the trials and triumphs of the struggle for independence and the challenge of building a new nation.

Frank Shuffelton, ed., *The Letters of John and Abigail Adams* (New York: Penguin Group, 2003). This collection of letters between John and Abigail Adams offers insight into American life before, during, and after the Revolution, as well as a glimpse into the Adamses' relationship, which spanned fifty-four years.

L. H. Butterfield, Marc Friedlaender, and Mary-Jo Kline, eds., *The Book of Abigail and John: Selected Letters of the Adams Family, 1762–1784* (Boston: Northeastern University Press, 2002). This book includes letters written by various members of the Adams family, particularly John and Abigail.

Lesson 8

NCSS Curriculum Standards

IV. Individual Development and Identity

Why do people behave as they do?

I. Culture

How do belief systems, such as religion or political ideals, influence culture?

II. Time, Continuity, and Change

What happened in the past, and how am I connected to those in the past?

V. Individuals, Groups, and Institutions

What are the roles of institutions in society?

VI. Power, Authority, and Governance

How are governments created, structured, and changed?

III. People, Places, and Environments

How did settlement patterns affect transmission of culture?

X. Civic Ideals and Practices

What is the role of a citizen?

Performance Expectations

Students will be able to:

1. Relate capabilities, learning, motivation, personality, and behavior to individual development.

2. Compare and analyze societal patterns for transmitting culture while adapting to social change.

3. Identify and use concepts such as causality and change to show connections among patterns of historical change and continuity.

4. Evaluate the role of institutions in furthering both continuity and change.

5. Describe the purpose of government and how its powers are acquired, used, and justified.

6. Examine, interpret, and analyze cultural patterns, such as cultural transmission of customs and ideas.

7. Analyze citizen action as it influences public policy.

Lesson 8:
Noah Webster

Questions to Ask Yourself throughout This Unit

- What attributes enabled Noah Webster to labor more than twenty years on his dictionary?

- What core beliefs led to Webster's convictions that the new nation needed an American system of elementary education that promoted patriotism and unity?

- What lessons can students today learn from an eighteenth-century country teacher?

Fasten Your Seat Belt

Unity, *U'NITY, n. [L. unitas.]*
1. The state of being one; oneness.
2. Agreement; uniformity; as unity of doctrine; unity of worship in a church.

This is a definition from the 1828 edition of Webster's dictionary, a massive work penned by Noah Webster. *Unity* is a word that expressed Noah Webster's goal for the United States.

Today, Americans often use Webster's dictionary, but rarely do they consider the years of labor and hard work that went into it. At the time Webster produced his small, simple dictionary (America's first) in 1806, dictionaries were rare. Following the publication of that early dictionary, Webster spent the next two decades completing his masterpiece—the comprehensive Webster's dictionary that is still famous today. In the years between publishing those dictionaries, Webster traveled across the world and learned more than twenty different languages. He wanted to be able to determine whether each word being defined had its roots in French, Latin, Russian, Arabic, or some other language. Webster published his comprehensive dictionary in 1828. It contained a total of seventy thousand words, including twelve thousand words and forty thousand definitions not found in any previous dictionary. Webster's dictionary unified and standardized the American version of the English language and thus had a significant impact on the country itself. As one work noted in 1845, shortly after his death:

Webster . . . has left us a standard of the English language which will guide all successive ages. . . . Noah Webster is the all-shaping, all-controlling mind of this hemisphere. He grew up with his country and he molded the intellectual character of her people. Not a man has sprung from her soil on whom he has not laid his all-forming hand. His principles of language have tinged every sentence that is now, or will ever be uttered by an American tongue.

Although Webster is known today primarily for his great dictionary, he impacted our country in many other ways. He was a judge, a legislator, a writer, an educator, and a soldier in the American Revolution. He joined other Founding Fathers in defining the governmental structures of a new nation; his efforts directly affected the content of the U.S. Constitution, and his writings motivated citizens to accept the plan of government outlined in the Constitution.

A Look in the Rearview Mirror
Marching to a Different Tune

The snappy melody of "Yankee Doodle" echoed across the Yale campus as undergraduates dashed into a militia formation. Discarding their silk educational robes and hats, quickly replacing them with military attire, the students lined up and practiced marching on the green. Meanwhile, Webster paced the company with patriotic tunes on his flute. Their practice was not in vain, for on June 29, 1775, the students joined with the New Haven militia to escort newly appointed commander in chief George Washington through town. The British army had invaded America just months before, and the Continental Congress had chosen General Washington to build an American army. The American Revolution was officially underway.

Webster had entered Yale College in 1774, when he was only sixteen years old. Over the next three years, the Revolutionary War threatened the academic flow at Yale; classes were disrupted and suspended on several occasions. Twice, Webster left Yale to join the local militia as they went to fight the British. The first occasion was in 1776, and the second was in 1777, when he joined his father and two older brothers in a march with the militia toward Albany, New York, to protect the region from the British. However, before the Websters arrived, Britain's General Burgoyne surrendered to General Gates at the Battle of Saratoga, resulting in America's first major victory in the American Revolution. Webster arrived too late to help with the fighting, but before returning to Yale to continue his academic studies, he assisted the army in gathering information about the five thousand British prisoners who had surrendered. Although Noah did not experience combat firsthand, he personally witnessed the difficulties of military life: Soldiers slept in smoke-filled tents to ward off mosquitoes; sicknesses such as dysentery and fever plagued the troops; the men lacked adequate food and clothing. Medical care was primitive, and death was not only frequent but also a long, agonizing process. Webster always remembered the human suffering that was required to secure American freedoms.

Detour: Title IX

When he was a schoolteacher, Noah Webster sponsored unprecedented programs to provide equal educational opportunities for women. Before the age of forty, he was considered one of the first American social reformers.

While the Revolution disrupted formal studies for Webster's graduating class of 1778, the political discussions surrounding the war provided an atmosphere of intellectual stimulation at the school. The talk of independence motivated the young Webster and his classmates, and the disruptions served as a catalyst for applying those thoughts.

The Yale faculty called off classes for other reasons besides disruptions caused by the Revolution. On one occasion, an epidemic of typhoid fever led to an extended dismissal of classes. Webster hurried home, where he found his older brother Abraham recovering from smallpox—a disease that in those days was often fatal. Such experiences stimulated Webster's thinking about medicine, and in 1800 he authored a two-volume medical work that was used as a textbook in medical schools and was considered the most important medical work written by someone outside the medical profession.

After Webster graduated from Yale, his interest in political matters continued. The Americans had won the Revolution, but they were not a unified nation. In fact, the form of government they had used during the Revolution (the Articles of Confederation) actually contributed to American disunity. Webster confronted this problem by speaking and writing about the need for a stronger federal government and national unity. In fact, he was one of the first Americans to call for a Constitutional Convention.

Webster was in Philadelphia at the time the Constitutional Convention met to address the problems of a weak central government. He regularly socialized with many of the delegates and participated in discussions with them about the weaknesses of the old government and the need for a new one. Some of his specific ideas were placed directly into the new Constitution, and when it was finished the delegates asked Webster to write an essay supporting the new form of government.

Webster's essay, which he dedicated to Benjamin Franklin, bolstered national support for the Constitution and greatly contributed to its eventual ratification and adoption by the states.

1. **What were two disruptions Yale students experienced in their education? How did these disruptions contribute to their education?**

Their education was disrupted by the Revolutionary War and by a typhoid fever epidemic. During the time off from classes, Noah Webster and his classmates received a practical education, learning firsthand about the difficulties of war and the need for improved medical practices. The events surrounding the Revolution also created an atmosphere of intellectual stimulation at the school and sparked discussion about independence among the students.

2. **Although Noah Webster did not actually fight in Revolutionary War battles, he still made contributions to the Patriot cause. List three of these contributions.**

He joined the militia and helped the troops handle the thousands of captured British soldiers from the Battle of Saratoga. He contributed to the national political discussion regarding the need for a stronger government. He was one of the first Americans to call for a constitutional convention. He rallied national support for the Constitution through his writing and speaking.

3. **Based on your knowledge of American history and the inference in the final paragraph above, what was the basic difference between the Articles of Confederation and the Constitution?**

The Articles of Confederation established a weak central government that provided individual states with such power that a state could veto the decisions of the rest of the states. The federal government therefore could not pass laws to collect taxes and did not have adequate power to create a unified nation. The Constitution provided a much stronger central government, which prevented a single state (or small group of states) from bringing government to a halt.

Historical Marker
Book Tour of the Century

After Noah Webster graduated from Yale, he returned home. His father, who had mortgaged the family farm in order to send his son to college, gave Noah an eight-dollar Continental note and said, "Take this; you must now seek your living; I can do no more for you." So young Webster secured his first job: He became a schoolteacher and embarked on a career that provided a platform from which he eventually would influence the entire nation.

As Webster walked four miles to and from the school he taught at each day, ideas for a completely new philosophy of education germinated in his mind. He realized that the students' textbooks relied too heavily on British materials. Americans had just finished a political revolution that separated them from Great Britain, and now they needed an educational revolution to separate themselves from the British system. Webster understood that a continued attachment to Great Britain in education might well lead to a similar return in politics. He argued, "America must be as independent in literature as she is in politics, as famous for arts as for arms." Webster's vision for America was a "system of elementary education by which the speech and language of the United States would be rendered uniform, moral and religious truths would be propagated, and a love of country would be developed." This was a revolutionary idea, and convincing others of the need for a purely American system of education would be a daunting task. But Webster accepted the challenge.

As part of his new education plan, Webster believed that American schools needed purely American textbooks. So he began writing such textbooks, and in 1782, he published America's first spelling book, in which he introduced the American spelling of words. For example, he used *labor, honor,* and *public* instead of the British spellings: *labour, honour, and publick*. The speller became one of the most famous books in American history; it was known as *The Blue-Back Speller* because it was often bound with a blue cover. (The speller is still used in some schools today.) To promote his American textbooks and vision for education, Webster traveled the country on horseback from New Hampshire

to South Carolina. As he crisscrossed the new nation, he stopped in city after city to promote *The Blue-Back Speller* and to give public lectures on the need for an American system of education. On his way, he met with university presidents and influential statesmen, seeking their suggestions and input. He also requested endorsements from national leaders. Webster spent a night at Mount Vernon in hopes of gaining support from the most important man in America: General George Washington.

During a series of lectures promoting his work, Webster met one of the country's famous statesmen, the aging Benjamin Franklin. A close friendship developed between the young author and the elder statesman as they discussed a mutual passion—a phonetic alphabet for the English language, which Webster had included in his spelling and grammar texts. They both agreed that the new nation needed a common speech to unify the republic and to mold the national character.

Webster's tour was only the beginning of his efforts to promote *The Blue-Back Speller*. He also advertised in newspapers, wrote press releases, donated the speller to charity events, and opposed his critics. Whenever his speller was attacked, he refuted every charge and submitted newspaper articles defending the book. The publicity surrounding the textbook resulted in huge sales.

The first edition of the speller had a print run of five thousand copies—a large printing in that day—and it sold out in less than a year (at fourteen cents per book!). Another edition was quickly printed, and it, too, promptly sold out. Edition after edition was printed and each sold out. The work sold so well that by 1810, two hundred editions had been printed, and eventually over 100 million copies were made. Unfortunately, because Webster always needed cash to print the new editions, he forfeited a fortune by requiring cash up front instead of earning royalties. Inadequate copyright laws and unscrupulous printers also hindered Webster, and finances plagued him his entire life. Nevertheless, his innovative marketing led to unparalleled success. Pioneers carried Webster's *Blue-Back Speller* across the country and printed an edition in the Oregon territory. And using only Webster's speller and its phonetic alphabet as a guide, a Cherokee named Sequoyah developed the first written language for his own people. From north to south, from the Atlantic to the Pacific, Webster's speller taught Americans to read. And incredibly, it also standardized the language they spoke, taught them moral and religious lessons, and unified the entire nation.

1. List three techniques that Noah Webster used to promote his book.

Webster elicited support and endorsements from influential American statesmen. He traveled throughout the country lecturing about his philosophy of education and the need for his speller. He advertised in newspapers, wrote press releases, and donated the speller to charity events. When criticism arose, he refuted the charges and defended his work.

2. Beyond the educational value of Webster's speller, what deeper significance did the text hold in the early years of the new nation?

As students across the nation used Webster's speller to learn spelling and reading, they embraced his spirit of patriotism and unity found in the examples he had included in the speller. The speller helped unite the country through a universal language and system of education. It played a part in the United States developing its own identity apart from Great Britain.

3. In what way was Noah Webster's role in the founding of our nation different from the roles of other Revolutionary heroes? Do you think this makes him any less of a Patriot than the others? Explain.

Answers will vary.

School Zone Ahead
Crossword Puzzle
(Language Arts Activity)

These definitions were taken from Webster's 1828 dictionary (which can be found online at www.cbtministries .org/resources/webster1828.htm). If you get stuck, use a modern dictionary and the helpful hints provided in italics.

Down

1. a tree of the genus *Ulmus* whose seed is called a samara
2. a vessel for containing oil to be burned by means of a wick; *today, a decorative appliance with a lightbulb and a shade*
4. government by the people
6. to praise; to extol; to commend
7. pits or excavations in the earth
8. understanding; the ability to learn and comprehend quickly
9. a commonwealth; a government in which the exercise of the sovereign power is lodged in representatives elected by the people
13. the edge or border of the mouth
14. plural of *I*
16. an expression of delight or regret
23. not employed; unoccupied with business
24. to soil; to sully; to contaminate; *today, can mean an insulting remark or a lack of enunciation in speech*
25. frozen vapor; watery particles congealed into white crystals in the air falling to earth
26. a line of light
27. a crowd or multitude of people who are rude, tumultuous, and disorderly without force
28. a connective that marks an alternative; *today, called a conjunction*

Across

3. a state or exemption from the power of another; liberty
5. faithful to a prince or superior
6. a shellfish with a bivalve
8. to make better
10. an image or representation
11. to use frugally; *can also serve as a term in bowling today*
12. an instrument used for writing; *in Webster's day, usually made from the quill of some large fowl*
13. rules
15. to support; to sustain; *also a type of large animal*
17. water or other fluid congealed [frozen] in a solid state
18. every one
19. lucky, fortunate, successful
20. to strike or touch either with or without force
21. the whole duration of a being
22. to look back on
27. the heavenly orb that revolves around the earth
29. one who computes or reckons; *today, an electronic device that performs mathematical calculations*
30. the objective case of *I*

¹E			²L			³F	R	E	E	D	⁴D	O	M
⁵L	O	Y	A	L							E		
M			M			⁶C	L	A	M		O		⁷M
	⁸I	M	P	⁹R	O	V	E				O		I
	N			E		L			¹⁰I	C	O	N	N
	T		¹¹S	P	A	R	E			R			E
¹²P	E	N		U		B		¹³L	¹⁴A	W	S		
	L		¹⁵B	E	¹⁶A	R		¹⁷I	C	E			
¹⁸A	L	L	L		H	A	P	P	Y				
	I		²⁰H	I	T		T						
²¹A	G	E	C		²²R	E	V	I	E	W			
	E		²³I		²⁴S					²⁵S			
	N		D		L	²⁶R		²⁷M	²⁸O	O	N		
	²⁹C	A	L	C	U	L	A	T	O	R			
³⁰M	E		E		R		Y		B		W		

Right of Way: Perseverance
According to Webster

The aging Patriot examined a definition in a Greek dictionary. Then he laid down the book, paced one step to his left, and picked up the French dictionary. Webster read the definition, pondered thoughtfully, and shuffled another pace clockwise around the semicircular table. He consulted texts in English, German, Hebrew, Arabic, Latin, Spanish, and other languages—twenty in all. He researched original meanings; he traced historical etymologies; he investigated word structures. He compared consonant and vowel relationships and recorded notes about his discoveries. Finally, with his curiosity satisfied and with a grasp of the basic meaning of the word, Webster then wrote down the definition. Hour after hour, day after day, year after year, he persisted in his meticulous endeavor, shedding light on each nuance of meaning. Throughout the years, every afternoon at four o'clock, Noah's wife, Rebecca, brought him a snack of fruit, nuts, or cake. He would finish the snack, then return to his work, again laboring diligently over every word.

Webster began work on his dictionary in 1800, and in 1806 he published the first American dictionary—a short, simple work that contained only the spellings of words but not their definitions. After publishing it, he continued working on word definitions. He finally completed the definition for his last word twenty-five years after he had begun! In January 1825 he wrote, "When I had come to the last word, I was seized with a trembling, which made it somewhat difficult to hold my pen steady for writing. . . . I summoned the strength to finish the last word, and then walking about the room a few minutes, I recovered."

From its inception, Noah Webster planned his dictionary as an *American* dictionary of the English language. The persistent sage wrote all seventy thousand words and their new definitions by hand. His patriotic nationalism wove its way throughout the work, highlighting both American culture and his belief that the brand-new nation already rivaled the centuries-old England in the area of literary achievement. And since Webster had declared early in the process that he intended his works to promote moral and religious truths as well as academic knowledge, it is not surprising that many definitions revealed Webster's Christian worldview.

Webster wanted a copy of his dictionary placed on the desk of every American teacher so that students would have ready access to this beacon of light and truth. Webster biographer Harry Warfel wrote, "The completion of the *Dictionary* was the feat of a preeminent scholar who had not forgotten his days of schoolmastering and who therefore continued to instruct his fellow citizens through the world's most important secular book."

From the beginning of the massive project, Webster had braved many obstacles: competitors made fun of his plans, and those who disagreed with his political views criticized his educational ideas and tried to ruin his creditability. He constantly faced financial pressures and even had to mortgage his home in order to publish his dictionary. But every bit of opposition only strengthened his resolve to light the way for future generations. That resolve eventually resulted in success.

Noah Webster published his last textbook when he was eighty-one years old. Within the pages of the text, he stressed the importance of persevering. When asked what contributed to his own remarkable vigor and long life, he listed four guidelines:

1. **Go to bed early and do not worry.**

2. **Get up early.**

3. **Exercise mentally and physically every day.**

4. **Keep a clear conscience void of offense toward God and man.**

Noah Webster's life ended the next year, in 1843. He had lived a lengthy and productive life, leaving a legacy as one of the most brilliant and well-informed men in U.S. history.

Webster's philosophy of learning altered educational practices in the new nation. His textbooks taught generations of American students to read and spell; his texts unified the speech and molded the character of citizens in the new American republic; and his patriotic ideas enlightened the country long after his death. In fact, the publishers of his 1845 speller (which Webster's son William helped get to press) summarized his extensive influence with these words: "Only two men have stood on the New World whose fame is so sure to last—Columbus, its discoverer; and Washington, its savior. Webster is and will be its great teacher; and these three make our trinity of fame."

The schoolbooks written by Webster enjoyed widespread use for decades after his death, and many of those texts featured a picture of Webster and a brief biography of this famous American. Above his picture appeared a phrase that aptly described Noah Webster's contributions and character: "Who taught millions to read, but not one to sin."

Defining Webster

If you had to choose one word that summed up Noah Webster's character, life experiences, and impact on American history, what word would you select? Copy the most fitting definition out of a dictionary, as well as the etymology of the word. Then explain why this word is an appropriate reflection of Webster's life.

Stop and Ponder

Noah Webster worked on his dictionary for a quarter of a century. Find someone who has worked at the same job for twenty-five years or more (or the longest period you're able to find). Develop a list of questions to ask this person, and then interview him or her.

You're in the Driver's Seat
Recognizing Bias

A worldview is a set of presuppositions or assumptions a person holds about the basic makeup of the world. These beliefs may be conscious or subconscious. Your worldview is a way of understanding the world and how you fit into the world you live in. Noah Webster operated from a Christian worldview, and his dictionary and textbooks reflect his beliefs and his assumptions about the world.

In our own reading, it is important to recognize that each author approaches a topic from a particular perspective and set of beliefs. Understanding an author's worldview helps us evaluate his or her writings.

With a small group or a partner, or on your own, complete the following activity to heighten your awareness of worldview and bias:

1. Identify various sources that report news in your community, such as local newspapers, weekly newsmagazines, Internet sites, radio programs, and local and national television news programs.

2. Choose a particular news event, and analyze the differences in the way various media sources report on it. Discuss instances of bias in the presentation of the news event.

3. What can you tell about the worldview of the author, reporter, or media source based on the article or report?

4. Think about your own worldview. How do you determine right and wrong?

Detour

In this definition from Webster's 1828 dictionary, you can see the etymology (origin) of the word, which traces its original use from a number of different languages, followed by definitions and illustrations from the Bible and other sources.

HEART, *n. h`art.* [Sax. *heort*; **G.** *herz*; **D.** *hart*; **Sw.** *heirta*; **Dan.** *hietre*; **Gr.** χαρδια; **Sans.** *herda.* I know not the primary sense, nor whether it is from the root of χεαρ, **L.** *cor, cordis,* and allied to **Eng.** *core,* or named from motion, pulsation.]

1. A muscular viscus, which is the primary organ of the blood's motion in an animal body, situated in the thorax. From this organ all the arteries arise, and in it all the veins terminate. By its alternate dilatation and contraction, the blood is received from the veins, and returned through the arteries, by which means the circulation is carried on and life preserved.

2. The inner part of any thing; the middle part or interior; as the *heart* of a country, kingdom or empire; the *heart* of a town; the *heart* of a tree.

3. The chief part; the vital part; the vigorous or efficacious part. *Bacon.*

4. The seat of the affections and passions, as of love, joy, grief, enmity, courage, pleasure, &c.

   The *heart* is deceitful above all things. Every imagination of the thoughts of the *heart* is evil continually. We read of an honest and good *heart,* and an evil *heart* of unbelief, a willing *heart,* a heavy *heart,* sorrow of *heart,* a hard *heart,* a proud *heart,* a pure *heart.* The *heart* faints in adversity, or under discouragement, that is courage fails; the *heart* is deceived, enlarged, reproved, lifted up, fixed, established, moved, &c. *Scripture.*

Worldview
Law: What Laws Rule Our Lives and Why?

In 1808, early during the Second Great Awakening (a national religious revival), Noah Webster experienced a religious conversion. As a result, he reevaluated all his basic beliefs, including his views on politics and education. In the areas of government and politics, his newfound faith in God only strengthened his earlier patriotic beliefs. As he explained to James Madison, "The Christian religion . . . is the basis—or rather the source—of all genuine freedom in government."

Detour
Each year new words are added to the Merriam-Webster dictionary. (For an online dictionary, see http://dictionary.reference.com.) Check out the following words and the year each was added to the dictionary.
body wrap—*a beauty treatment (1974)*
tweener—*a player who has some but not all of the necessary characteristics for each of two or more positions (as in football or basketball) (1978)*
darmstadtium—*a short-lived radioactive element produced artificially (1984)*
blog—*shorthand for Web log; a Web site that contains an online personal journal with reflections, comments, and often hyperlinks provided by the writer (2004)*
podcasting—*the Web-based broadcast of music, which works with software that automatically detects new files and is accessed by subscription (2004)*

> *"The Bible is the Chief moral cause of all that is good, and the best corrector of all that is evil, in human society; the best book for regulating the temporal concerns of men, and the only book that can serve as an infallible guide."*
> **Noah Webster**

Not only did Webster share the beneficial principles of religion with the nation, but he instilled in his own family a love and veneration for the Scriptures that he considered the greatest legacy he could leave them. In 1832, thirty-five of his children, grandchildren, and great-grandchildren gathered in New Haven to celebrate—three years late—Noah and Rebecca's golden wedding anniversary. Their daughter Eliza described what transpired on that day to confirm Noah's commitment to his legacy:

> *We all went to Father's and took our tea in the home of our early days. In the evening before we parted, our beloved and revered parent called our attention, and kneeling, as we all did, fervently implored the blessing of heaven upon us, our children, and our children's children to the latest generation. . . . Then rising, he said, it was the happiest day of his life to see us all together; so many walking in the truth; and the others, children of*

promise. . . . Then he presented each of us with a Bible—his last gift—with our names written by his own trembling hand. . . . Their little Bibles are cherished gifts.

"In my view, the Christian religion is the most important and one of the first things in which all children, under a free government ought to be instructed."
Noah Webster

After his years as a schoolteacher, Noah Webster became an attorney and a lawmaker, and he served as a legislator. His Christian faith and the Scriptures formed the foundation for his approach to law. As a result of his Christian worldview, a strong moral tone permeated his original dictionary. In its preface, Webster dedicated that great dictionary to God, announcing: "To that great and benevolent Being . . . Who has borne me and my manuscripts in safety across the Atlantic, and given me strength and resolution to bring the work to a close, I would present the tribute of my most grateful acknowledgments." He then offered the work to Americans: "I present [this dictionary] to my fellow-citizens . . . with my ardent wishes for their improvement and happiness and . . . the moral and religious elevation of character and the glory of my country."

Map Your Way

"The moral principles and precepts contained in the Scriptures ought to form the basis of all of our civil constitutions and laws."
Noah Webster

Before you drive any farther down the road of life, consider these questions:

⊚ **What "rules of the road" do you follow when you make decisions?**

⊚ **What legacy would you want to leave for your future children and grandchildren?**

"By associating with her, [he] must become a better man, a better citizen, a warmer friend. His heart must be softened by her virtues, his benevolent and tender affections must be multiplied. In short, he must be good, for he would be in some measure, like her."
Noah Webster, regarding his future wife, Rebecca, in a letter to her brother John

DVD Reflection

Watch the DVD segment for Lesson 8 and complete the following activities:

Noah Webster
Father of American Education

Three ways Webster unified the nation:

Three books Webster contributed during America's founding years:

Dave Stotts describes Noah Webster as a man who communicated the King's English with an American twist. See if you can unscramble the American and British spellings of these words:

balro/buarol
labor/labour

rlooc/luoorc
color/clour

lupbci/lukpbci
public/publick

ziralee/sliaree
realize/realise

ohorn/uhoorn
honor/honour

For Further Study

Geography

Yale College (now Yale University)
New Haven, Connecticut
Albany, New York
Philadelphia, Pennsylvania
Mount Vernon

Historical Context

Battle of Saratoga
Articles of Confederation
Constitutional Convention
Shays' Rebellion
Blue-Back Speller
Second Great Awakening

Significant Individuals and Groups

General John Burgoyne
General Horatio Gates
Sequoyah

Terms

militia
dysentery
epidemic
typhoid fever
smallpox
ratification
phonetics
copyright
etymology
worldview

Additional Resources

Harry Warfel, *Noah Webster, Schoolmaster to America* (New York: Macmillan, 1936). This comprehensive biography, which was reprinted in 1966, traces the stages of Webster's life and champions his contributions toward building a unified nation.

David Sargent, *Noah Webster* (Hartford, Conn.: The Noah Webster Foundation and Historical Society of West Hartford, Inc., 1976). Sargent's book is a short biography highlighting many of Webster's talents and contributions to American culture.

http://www.cbtministries.org/resources/webster1828.htm. This online version of Webster's 1828 dictionary offers a search engine to look up definitions of words as they would have appeared in the original text.

Lesson 9

NCSS Curriculum Standards

IV. Individual Development and Identity

Why do people behave as they do?

I. Culture

How do belief systems, such as religion or political ideals, influence culture?

II. Time, Continuity, and Change

What happened in the past, and how am I connected to those in the past?

VIII. Science, Technology, and Society

How can we preserve our fundamental values and beliefs in the midst of technological change?

IX. Global Connections

How do age-old ethnic enmities impact human rights?

Performance Expectations

Students will be able to:

1. Identify and describe the influence of attitudes, values, and beliefs on personal identity.

2. Interpret patterns of behavior reflecting values and attitudes that contribute to cross-cultural understanding.

3. Investigate, interpret, and analyze multiple historical viewpoints across cultures related to important events while employing empathy, skepticism, and critical judgment.

4. Make judgments about how science and technology have transformed human society and our understanding of time, space, place, and human-environment interactions.

5. Demonstrate understanding of concerns, standards, issues, and conflicts related to universal human rights.

Lesson 9:
John Quincy Adams

Questions to Ask Yourself throughout This Unit

- What attributes worked to both the advantage and disadvantage of John Quincy Adams?

- On what core beliefs did he refuse to compromise in his political and personal decisions?

Fasten Your Seat Belt

Have you ever felt like you didn't quite fit in—like you were an outsider from the rest of the group? Have you ever been disliked because of your opinions or criticized because of your decisions? If so, you will relate to John Quincy Adams.

Although John Quincy Adams achieved the honor of becoming the sixth president of the United States, both his own political party and his opponents' party disliked him. He often refused to do what either of them wanted, choosing instead to do what he believed was right for America. By the end of his term, John Quincy Adams was known as "the most unpopular president," a nickname that would make anyone want to give up. But not President Adams. In fact, the same persistent, independent, and steadfast spirit that caused him to be disliked as president helped him become one of America's most effective and honored legislators.

131

When false allegations were brought against the Adamses in pro-Jackson newspapers, John Quincy's wife, Louisa, wrote a direct rebuttal of the story. It was the first time a woman in her position responded in such a bold, confrontational manner to false charges in the national media.

At an age when most men are retiring, the sixty-four-year-old former president began a new and highly successful career—he was elected to the U.S. House of Representatives. (Adams was the only president ever to serve in Congress after his presidency.) He served for seventeen years in that position, until his death. His success in Congress made him an American legend and earned him a *new* nickname. No longer was he America's most unpopular president; he became known as "Old Man Eloquent"—one of the nation's best orators, known especially for his outspoken and compelling speeches against slavery. At the end of Adams's long career, Massachusetts Governor Edward Everett told the public: "The traits which formed the heroism of his character and . . . made him at all times and in any career a person of the highest mark and force were his lion-heart (which knew not the fear of man) and his religious spirit (which feared God in all things). . . . A person of truer courage, physical and moral, I think never lived."

A Look in the Rearview Mirror
Adventure at Sea

In the winter of 1777, ten-year-old John Quincy Adams, known as Johnny, embarked on the ultimate boyhood adventure. Johnny's father, Congressman John Adams, had been appointed the United States commissioner to France. While his mother, Abigail Adams, and the rest of the family stayed home to take care of the homestead, Johnny (the eldest son) accompanied his father to his new job in France. It would be three long years before Johnny saw his mother, brothers, and sister again, but during that time Abigail kept up a regular correspondence with both her husband and her son, and she faithfully prayed for them both.

Any voyage across the ocean was hazardous in those days, but Johnny's trip to France was especially dangerous for two reasons: First, the harsh Boston winter would make sailing treacherous, and second, crossing in wartime brought incredible risks, particularly since the enemy was specifically looking for John Adams. Yet in order to assume his new responsibilities across the ocean, John Adams was forced to sail as quickly as possible. Their three-thousand-mile voyage across the North Atlantic was delayed for two days due to blinding snowstorms and chilling fourteen-degree temperatures. Then, on a day filled with winds at gale force, John Adams, his son Johnny, and their servant Joseph Stephens boarded the brand-new twenty-four-gun frigate *Boston*, under the command of Captain Samuel Tucker. To avoid both the British spies around Boston and the enemy cruisers in New England waters, the ship left during the night. All this secrecy and the threat of captivity conjured up a "thousand fears" for Johnny's mother, Abigail. For a ten-year-old boy it must have been like being in the pages of a *Robinson Crusoe* adventure.

Once the great vessel set sail, Johnny took to following the salty, booming-voiced Captain Tucker around the *Boston*. With the captain's help, Johnny learned the names of each sail and mastered the use of a mariner's compass.

During Adams's terms in Congress, his wife, Louisa, was one of his most passionate aides. When he was flooded with antislavery petitions, it was Louisa who read, filed, and cataloged these petitions.

The voyage wasn't always smooth sailing—sea travel was extremely treacherous even in the best of times. The typical voyage between the two continents lasted from six to twelve weeks. Passengers were often afflicted with diseases and faced difficulties such as leaky vessels and unfavorable weather. In 1750, not long before Johnny embarked on his voyage, one German immigrant described his own crossing of the Atlantic:

During the voyage, there is on board these ships terrible misery, stench, fumes, horror, vomiting, many kinds of seasickness, fever, dysentery, headache, heat, boils, scurvy, cancer, mouth rot, and the like, all of which come from old and sharply-salted food and meat, also from very bad and foul water, so that many die miserably.
. . . Children from one to seven years rarely survive the voyage; and many-

a-time parents are compelled to see their children miserably suffer and die from hunger, thirst, and sickness, and then to see them cast into [buried in] the water. I witnessed such misery in no less than thirty-two children in our ship, all of whom were thrown into [buried in] the sea.

The voyage undertaken by Johnny and his father was by no means safe. In fact, one night when the ship was struck by violent storms, Johnny's father wrote that the ship, "shuddered . . . [and] darted from side to side . . . all hands were called [on deck]. It was with the utmost difficulty that my little son and I could hold ourselves in bed with both our hands, . . . bracing ourselves against the boards . . . with our feet." After the storm settled, John Adams wrote in his diary about Johnny's bravery: "Fully sensible of our danger, he was constantly endeavoring to bear up under it with manly courage and patience." Also during the crossing, British warships drew near, and John Adams took to the rigging with rifle in hand, prepared to defend the ship.

During the six-week voyage to France, Johnny's father also made sure that he continued his formal education, including lessons from the Bible. One course was taught by an unexpected source: a fellow traveler. French surgeon Nicolas Noel spoke English and liked Johnny so much that he taught him French. A few years later, Johnny's proficiency in French helped win him the honor of being the youngest diplomat in American history. Although he was only eleven years old, Johnny received a congressional diplomatic appointment as the official secretary to his father, John Adams, ambassador to France. Johnny's knowledge of French proved invaluable in that position. Three years later, Congress appointed the fourteen-year-old Johnny as the secretary to Francis Dana, the ambassador to the court of Catherine the Great in Russia. When Johnny was sixteen years old, President George Washington called him "the most valuable character we have abroad," predicting of the young Adams that he "will prove himself to be the ablest of all our diplomatic corps."

Although as an adult John Quincy Adams became an accomplished writer, a brilliant scholar, and an outstanding attorney, he was destined for one career from childhood—a career that would require unusual courage—that of a statesman. He was a child of the American Revolution who had witnessed firsthand the Battle of Bunker Hill, the fall of the Dutch Republic, and Napoleon's invasion of Russia. Johnny grew up surrounded by many of America's greatest heroes: George Washington, Thomas Jefferson, Benjamin Franklin, Samuel Adams, John Hancock, and Marquis de Lafayette.

Yet the foundation for the remarkable accomplishments of his long life was his upright character—a character formed during his childhood. His parents raised him with a deep respect for God and an equally strong love for his country; he never abandoned either. In fact, when he was seventy-eight years old (only a year before his death), he reminisced about his mother's training:

My mother was the daughter of a Christian clergyman. . . . In that same spring and summer of 1775 [when I was seven], she taught me to repeat daily after the Lord's Prayer (before rising from bed) the "Ode to Collins" on the patriot warriors [a poem of patriotism]. . . . Of the impression made upon my heart by the sentiments inculcated [instilled] in these beautiful effusions [outpourings] of patriotism and poetry, you may form an estimate by the fact that now—seventy-one years after they were thus taught me—I repeat them from memory.

Abigail valued moral and religious character so much that after ten-year-old Johnny arrived in France, she wrote him, "Dear as you are to me, I would much rather you should have found your grave in the ocean you have just crossed than see you an immoral, profligate [rebellious], or graceless child."

Johnny's solid character, assorted experiences, and willingness to learn equipped him to become a noted American diplomat. He was an ambassador to five different nations, under three different presidents. He served as a Massachusetts legislator, U.S. senator, university professor, U.S. president, and U.S. congressman. Additionally, he became an author and a noted poet, frequently penning religious poems.

Throughout his distinguished political career, John Quincy Adams often related braving the storms aboard the *Boston* as a child to the storminess of politics he faced as an adult. Although Adams sailed to and from Europe many more times, there was never an ocean voyage comparable to his first. Adams loved to recall the savage storms, the battles at sea, the misery and terror— the exhilarating adventure of it all.

1. How did the hard times John Quincy Adams experienced in his early days benefit him later in his life?

John Quincy Adams's principled upbringing, dangerous travels, and exposure to various worldwide crises molded his character and prepared him to stand for what was right despite adversity, criticism, and pressure. His experiences taught him skills he would need to serve his country in the future, including foreign languages, diplomacy, and courage.

2. Compare and contrast the educational experiences of John Quincy Adams to your own.

3. John Quincy Adams's mother encouraged him to memorize the Lord's Prayer and the patriotic poem "Ode to Collins." Choose a poem, song, or other work, and spend the next week committing it to memory. If you're having trouble making a selection, you might want to consider "The Star-Spangled Banner," Ralph Waldo Emerson's "Concord Hymn," or Walt Whitman's "O Captain! My Captain!"

Stop and Ponder (for Group Discussion)

Describe "storms" in your life that have worked out for good.

Tell about one of the most exciting adventures you've experienced. How do your adventures compare to those of John Quincy Adams?

Historical Marker
Seat No. 203 in the U.S. Congress

For many Americans, becoming president of the United States would be the ultimate career. Yet for John Quincy Adams, despite having served a term as president, the job title he relished most was "U.S. Representative Adams in Seat No. 203 in the U.S. Congress." This second career qualifies him as the only ex-president ever elected to the House of Representatives. And at the time, it caused quite a stir. For someone to become a congressman after serving as president just wasn't done; this unconventional order was seen as belittling—almost like the master of the house becoming the butler or maid. But President Adams didn't care what others thought of him or what was expected. Regarding his election to Congress, he wrote, "No election or appointment ever gave me so much pleasure. My election as president was not half as gratifying." Not only was his role as a congressman his favorite job, but it also fit his personality perfectly. He held that post at a time in history when he was able to have a great impact on the future of the United States.

The road to political success for Adams was paved with speed bumps and potholes. When he was elected president, he received such a narrow majority of votes that the decision went before the House of Representatives; there he won the presidency by only one vote. Although he did not have a broad base of support, John Quincy Adams was nevertheless inaugurated as America's sixth president in 1825, at the age of fifty-seven. He was the first son to follow in his father's footsteps as president. (His father was America's second president.)

Although John Quincy Adams had been raised in and around the political world, the training he received from his parents led to the development of his strong and unwavering character.

His early lessons remained with him throughout his public service. As a result, he was a nonconformist who cared less about what people thought of him than what was right or wrong. He placed little emphasis on what he considered to be superficial or inconsequential matters. For example, his critics claimed that he was the most shabbily dressed man ever to have sat in the presidential chair, and one tradition claims that he wore the same hat in Washington for ten years! He was more concerned with what was comfortable than with the latest fashion trends. And since John Quincy Adams enjoyed playing billiards with his son, he became the first president to have a pool table in the White House. He was harshly criticized for this, because many people considered billiards, along with other forms of gambling, a sin. Adams was indeed concerned about sin, for he was a deeply committed and outspoken Christian. In fact, in 1848, his letters to his ten-year-old son training him to understand and love the Bible were published as a book to benefit all young Americans. Adams also served as a vice president of the American Bible Society. In Adams's careful study of the Bible, he saw no basis for the charge that playing billiards with his son was a sin; therefore, he ignored what his critics said about him.

When John Quincy's wife, Louisa, died, both houses of Congress adjourned for the day of her funeral. She was the first woman to be honored in this way.

With all the criticism that Adams received during his presidency, it is not surprising that when it came time for reelection, Andrew Jackson easily defeated him. When Adams left Washington, most Americans assumed he was finished with public service. Yet nothing was further from the truth. There was no notion of quitting in him. He reentered politics as a congressman and loved the position so much that he declared he hoped to die in the pursuit of duty. In 1848, he suffered a stroke on the floor of the House and died two days later inside the Capitol building.

Enemies who strongly differed with Adams on various issues still respected him as a person. Although Adams was their opponent, they knew him as a man of integrity who was thoroughly truthful and who always did what he believed to be right. Once when Congress was split and neither side was able to elect a Speaker of the House, both sides agreed to let John Quincy Adams serve as speaker until the dispute was resolved. They all knew that he was completely fair, just, and honest.

Adams's unwillingness to compromise on right and wrong made him a perfect champion for important moral issues of the day. He adamantly opposed slavery. His outspoken view on this issue brought him harsh criticism and more than a dozen death threats. Most members of the House were proslavery, so Adams lost nearly every antislavery measure he introduced. Nevertheless, he persisted, and they nicknamed him the "hellhound of abolition" for his relentless, bulldog-like tenacity. Although he suffered numerous defeats, Adams never gave up, because he had adopted the philosophy "Duty is ours; results are God's." He was determined to always do what was right and leave the outcome to God. In speeches he often quoted from the Bible to justify his position that slavery is wrong and should be ended.

In 1841, with bad eyesight and trembling hands, Adams, seventy-four, used his skills as an attorney to fight slavery. While most attorneys before the Supreme Court today are allowed to speak for only thirty minutes, Adams delivered a speech that lasted nine hours and spanned three days. He defended thirty-nine Africans who had seized the slave ship *Amistad*. (This story has been told in the movie *Amistad*.) Although the Supreme Court at the time was strongly proslavery, Adams won the case. After a dozen years of butting heads with Adams, most of the representatives in the House finally converted to his antislavery position. His fellow House members awarded him an engraved walking cane celebrating changes he had brought about in the House. (That cane is now in the Smithsonian museum in Washington DC.)

By the time of his death, John Quincy Adams had been reelected to Congress eight times. One of his admirers, minister and poet Ralph Waldo Emerson, summed up the feelings of many when he called Adams "a bruiser who loved a good fight." His bruiserlike, uncompromising tendencies played an important role in securing the freedom and equality that we experience in the United States today.

Choose one of the activities below about the life of John Quincy Adams:

1. **Nickname Cartoon**
   Create a political cartoon (with illustrations and captions) that depicts one or more of the nicknames John Quincy Adams received throughout his career: "the most unpopular president," "Old Man Eloquent," "a bruiser who loved a good fight," "a bulldog among spaniels," or "hellhound of abolition."

2. **"Graffitied" Walking Cane**
   Using wood, papier-mâché, or some other medium, create a rough replica of the walking cane that John Quincy Adams's fellow House members had engraved for him. Be sure to include on it changes he brought about during his service to the United States.

3. **Presidential Poetry**
   One of John Quincy Adams's admirers was the poet Ralph Waldo Emerson. Emerson used vivid language to describe the former president and statesman. Write a poem yourself reflecting on Adams's contributions to American history.

Stop and Ponder (for Group Discussion)

How do the opinions of other people affect your behavior? When is it good and when is it harmful to be influenced by others?

When you don't succeed at something the first time, how do you respond?

Right of Way: Determination
Doggedly Guarding the Smithsonian

Where can we find items that represent America's history? The scarecrow's costume from *The Wizard of Oz,* Muhammad Ali's boxing glove, Thomas Edison's lightbulb, George Washington's uniform, and Lewis and Clark's compass can all be found in one of the most-visited public places in the world: the Smithsonian Institution, which houses sixteen museums and galleries, as well as the National Zoo. Yet if it were not for one determined congressman with a vision for a better America, there would be no Smithsonian.

When John Quincy Adams gave his State of the Union address in 1825, he proposed the radical idea that the government should support science and culture; he also suggested that the United States start a national university, send out an exploring expedition, and build an observatory. His audience was shocked—as dumbfounded as if he had proposed visiting the moon! Many of his opponents criticized him and mocked his ideas. There was simply no interest among government leaders in investing for the future, whether in observatories or museums.

But just as Adams doggedly opposed slavery, he also continued to champion his idea for a national museum. In 1829, wealthy Englishman James Smithson, who had never visited America, died and left his entire fortune (half a million dollars) to the United States of America. It was one of the largest sums of money donated to the American government in the nineteenth century—and also one of the most mysterious. He designated that the large sum of money, which would be equivalent to $50 million today, be used "to found . . . an establishment for the increase and diffusion of knowledge among men." Adams recognized Smithson's donation as the opportunity to finally see the United States advance in science and culture, and he felt it was his personal responsibility to guard

the money for its intended purpose. Adams recorded his enthusiasm about Smithson's bequest: "I see the finger of Providence, compassing great results by incomprehensible means."

Most Americans resisted using the money for a museum, and Adams at times felt discouraged about the fate of Smithson's money. However, the thought of giving up never lingered long in John Quincy Adams's mind. He tirelessly presented his views again and again. One of his enemies described Congressman John Quincy Adams as "a bulldog among spaniels." Shortly before his death, Adams saw his dream of the Smithson bequest become reality. On August 10, 1846, President James K. Polk signed the bill creating the Smithsonian Institution (which passed by only nine votes). Because of John Quincy Adams's determination to plan for the future, the treasures of American history have a permanent home in the Smithsonian.

Adams's vision of having national observatories also became reality before he died. In 1842, the U.S. Naval Observatory was finally founded in Washington as a place for scientists to study the stars and the heavens. In 1843, when an observatory was built in Cincinnati that housed the largest

refracting telescope in the country, John Quincy Adams laid the cornerstone.

1. **Discuss the meaning of the description of Adams as "a bulldog among spaniels."**

Bulldogs are a breed of dogs known for their courage, tenacity, and stubbornness in standing their ground against attack. Spaniels, on the other hand, are generally known for their friendly temperaments. They rarely defend their ground and are happy to go along with whoever pays attention to them, be it friend or enemy.

2. **List two contributions resulting from Adams's determination that have benefited future generations.**

(1) Due in large part to Adams's unwillingness to allow the Smithson fortune to be spent on any other project, the Smithsonian Institution has become the principal cultural institution of the United States. The tenacity and grit of John Quincy Adams secured the funds for these museums, and future generations continue to benefit from his contributions. (2) Today the entire country benefits from the naval observatory and astronomical programs first proposed by Adams. (3) John Quincy Adams's ardent efforts to end slavery, while unsuccessful in his own lifetime, contributed greatly to the national efforts that eventually and successfully ended that heinous institution. His positive effect on Abraham Lincoln is one illustration of Adams's enduring influence on future generations.

3. **If James Smithson could see the Smithsonian Institution today, what do you think his reaction would be? How successful do you think the Smithsonian has been in fulfilling his hope of increasing knowledge?**

Answers will vary.

4. **What did Adams mean when he said, "I see the finger of Providence, compassing great results by incomprehensible means"?**

Adams believed that God was guiding and directing human events—even through unusual means—ultimately to accomplish what was good for the United States through having Smithson's bequest achieve its intended object.

Detour: A Man of Influence

An often unnoticed but significant antislavery accomplishment made by John Quincy Adams was the profound influence he had as a mentor on a new congressman from Illinois. This legislator served only two years in the House of Representatives, and both before and after those two years in Congress, his life was marked by defeat. He failed in business and lost races for the state legislature, U.S. House, and U.S. Senate. Yet for one brief term, the inexperienced man served in the U.S. House of Representatives alongside the elderly John Quincy Adams, who was in his final term of office. Adams's influence on the freshman congressman during that short time was so great that when Adams died, the young legislator served as one of Adams's pallbearers. That congressman was Abraham Lincoln. And the two years Lincoln spent beside John Quincy Adams influenced the future president mightily. When Lincoln was elected president of the United States two decades later, many of the measures he initiated to end slavery were in line with earlier recommendations made by John Quincy Adams. Adams's influence on Abraham Lincoln proved to be providential for America.

School Zone Ahead

The Smithsonian Institution (Research and Technology Activity)

When James Smithson left his library, mineral collection, and entire fortune to the United States in 1829, he surely could not have imagined the establishment that today bears his name: the Smithsonian Institution. The world's largest museum complex is made up of fifteen different museums. The mission of the Smithsonian Institution is "the increase and diffusion of knowledge." Log on to the Smithsonian Web site at www.si.edu to explore the museum and discover treasures of our nation.

Your teacher will assign you and your partner one of the following museums that make up the Smithsonian Institution: Anacostia Museum, Arts and Industries Building; Cooper-Hewitt, National Design Museum; Freer Gallery of Art and Arthur M. Sackler Gallery; Hirshhorn Museum and Sculpture Garden; National Air and Space Museum; National Museum of African Art; National Museum of American History, Behring Center; National Museum of Natural History; National Museum of the American Indian; National Portrait Gallery; National Postal Museum; National Zoological Park; Smithsonian American Art Museum and Renwick Gallery; or Smithsonian Institution Building (the Castle).

1. With a partner, investigate the museum assigned to you.

2. Make a poster with four to six segments. Include information about the following:

- a brief explanation of the museum

- five American treasures a visitor to this museum might view

- one interesting fact you learned from researching the museum

- a critique of how effectively this particular museum fulfills Smithson's request that the establishment "increase . . . knowledge among men."

3. Include pictures on your poster (printed or original) that correspond with each section of the poster.

4. Share your poster with the class.

You're in the Driver's Seat
Standing Firm

The movie *Amistad*, directed by Steven Spielberg, is based on the 1839 revolt of Africans on the Spanish slave ship *Amistad*. Former president John Quincy Adams argued the case before the U.S. Supreme Court in 1841. His arguments eventually led to a settlement that awarded these individuals their freedom.

⚙ **John Quincy Adams never wavered in his advocacy for human rights. What do you consider to be worth fighting for?**

⚙ **What gives a fight value?**

Worldview
Ethics: How Do I Know What's Right or Wrong?

John Quincy Adams's death resulted in a time of national mourning; the nation honored the life of one of its greatest statesmen. Voices across the country recalled the remarkable character and great contributions of President Adams. Timothy Walker, a judge and founder of the Cincinnati Law School, summed up the opinions of many Americans regarding John Quincy Adams when he said, "He aimed to be a Christian statesman—and I regard this as the resplendent glory of his life. No earthly consideration ever could, or did, make him swerve from what he thought to be his duty."

Map Your Way
"From the day of the Declaration . . . they [the American people] were bound by the laws of God . . . and by the laws of The Gospel, which they nearly all, acknowledge as the rules of their conduct."
John Q. Adams

The statement above came from John Quincy Adams's July 4, 1821, Independence Day speech. In that speech, he declared that the American people acknowledged the Bible as the rule book for conducting their lives. Certainly, the Bible provided the moral framework from which John Quincy Adams made ethical decisions. He considered these standards to be unchanging truths—absolutes that provided guidelines for almost every situation. As you map out the trail for your life, consider these questions:

⚙ **How do you make ethical decisions about what is right and wrong?**

⚙ **Are your standards of right and wrong based on absolutes, or are they relative—subject to change depending on the circumstances?**

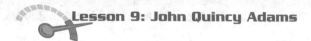

DVD Reflection

Watch the DVD segment for Lesson 9 and complete the following activities:

John Quincy Adams
Old Man Eloquent

As you watch, jot down three of John Quincy Adams's accomplishments and how old he was when he did each one.

Accomplishment	Age
1.	
2.	
3.	

Use the flow chart to show how one of John Quincy Adams's experiences paved the way for future service to his country.

Experience

Action

Result

An engraved walking cane given to John Quincy Adams by his fellow House members is now in the Smithsonian Institution. If the Smithsonian were to house one symbol representing your life, what would it be?

For Further Study

Geography
France
Boston, Massachusetts
Smithsonian Institution
U.S. Naval Observatory

Historical Context
Battle of Bunker Hill
American Bible Society
Supreme Court

Significant Individuals and Groups
Edward Everett
Samuel Tucker
Nicolas Noel
Francis Dana
Catherine the Great
Napoleon
Andrew Jackson
Ralph Waldo Emerson
Abraham Lincoln
James Smithson
James K. Polk
Timothy Walker

Terms
eloquent
commissioner
gale
frigate
mariner's compass
scurvy
mouth rot
diplomat
ambassador
nonconformist
Speaker of the House
abolition
bequest
refracting telescope
absolutes

Additional Resources

Leonard L. Richards, *The Life and Times of Congressman John Quincy Adams* (New York: Oxford University Press, 1986). This biography examines John Quincy Adams's role as a congressman and his rise to status as a political folk hero as he opposed slavery and became known as the conscience of New England.

Edward Everett, *A Eulogy on the Life and Character of John Quincy Adams* (Boston: Dutton and Wentworth, 1848). This eulogy was delivered at the request of the legislature of Massachusetts in Faneuil Hall on April 15, 1848.

Nina Burleigh, *The Stranger and the Statesman: James Smithson, John Quincy Adams, and the Making of America's Greatest Museum: The Smithsonian* (New York: HarperCollins Publishers Inc., 2003). This book tells the unusual story surrounding the creation of the Smithsonian Institution.

Amistad (1997 movie). This 152-minute movie depicts the powerful courtroom defense of John Quincy Adams as he argues in favor of freeing Africans who rebelled on a slave ship. The initial scenes include graphic violence as the African slaves overthrow their captors. This movie is rated R for scenes of strong brutal violence and some related nudity, so it may not be appropriate for students. However, you might consider showing an excerpt related to John Quincy Adams. As with all material, it is wise to preview movies to determine their appropriateness for your class.

National Council for the Social Studies Standards

Lesson 1

Thematic Strands and Primary Questions	Performance Expectations	Student Questions
	Faith and Freedom, History	
II. Time, Continuity, and Change — What happened in the past, and how am I connected to those in the past?	Systematically employ processes of critical historical inquiry, such as using a variety of sources and checking their credibility, validating and weighing evidence for claims, and searching for causality.	How did the Founders understand the relationship between church and state?
V. Individuals, Groups, and Institutions — What are the roles of institutions in society?	Identify and describe examples of tensions between belief systems and government policies and laws.	How did the plan of government outlined in the Mayflower Compact differ from the English government?
VI. Power, Authority, and Governance — How are governments created, structured, and changed? How can individual rights be protected within the context of majority rule?	Analyze and explain ideas and mechanisms to meet needs and wants of citizens, regulate territory, manage conflict, establish order and security, and balance competing conceptions of a just society.	When we compare primary and secondary sources, are the original meanings altered?
IX. Global Connections — How do we balance the tension between national interests and global priorities?	Describe instances in which language, art, belief systems, and other cultural elements can facilitate understanding or cause misunderstanding.	How did the governments designed by Pilgrims and Puritans (including Roger Williams and Anne Hutchinson) differ?
X. Civic Ideals and Practices — How has the meaning of citizenship evolved?	Explain the origins and interpret the continuing influence of key ideals of the democratic republican form of government.	How can a religiously diverse nation balance respect for all backgrounds with its moral foundation?

Lesson 2

Thematic Strands and Primary Questions	Performance Expectations	Student Questions
	Benjamin Franklin, Philosophy	
I. Culture How do belief systems, such as religion or political ideals, influence culture?	Identify the values and virtues of Benjamin Franklin, and describe ways his beliefs and attitudes helped shape our country.	How did the values and virtues of Benjamin Franklin shape the new American nation?
V. Individuals, Groups, and Institutions What are the roles of institutions in society, how am I influenced by institutions, and what is my role in institutional change?	Apply knowledge of how groups and institutions, such as those designed by Benjamin Franklin, work to meet individual needs and promote the common good.	How did Franklin's organizational abilities and interactions with others promote the common good?
VIII. Science, Technology, and Society How can we manage technology so that the greatest number of people benefit from it?	Identify historical examples of the interaction and interdependence of science, technology, and society, and seek reasonable and ethical solutions to problems that arise when scientific advancements and social norms or values come into conflict.	How did Benjamin Franklin's scientific experiments transform society?
II. Time, Continuity, and Change What happened in the past, and how am I connected to those in the past?	Identify and apply lessons from Franklin's life to their own experiences.	What twenty-first century lessons can this eighteenth century man teach?

Lesson 3

Thematic Strands and Primary Questions	Ex—rmance ...ns Benjamin R... Sociology	Student Questions
I. Culture How do belief systems, such as religion or political ideals, influence culture?	Compare and contrast the way different groups meet human needs and concerns.	shap—principles and beliefs Rush? Wh...do we learn about his chara...r and motives from the wa, he approached medicine and interacted with people?
IV. Individual Development and Identity Why do people behave as they do, and how do individuals develop from youth to adulthood?	Describe the ways religion, gender, ethnicity, and socioeconomic status contribute to the development of a sense of self.	What attributes helped Benjamin Rush stand firm under difficult circumstances?
V. Individuals, Groups, and Institutions What are the roles of institutions in society, how am I influenced by institutions, and what is my role in institutional change?	Describe the role of institutions in furthering both continuity and change.	What foundational institutions are needed for a healthy society?
X. Civic Ideals and Practices How has the meaning of citizenship evolved, and what is the balance between rights and responsibilities?	Examine the origins and continuing influence of key ideals of the democratic republican form of government, such as individual human dignity, liberty, justice, and equality.	How do you respond when you see an underdog? What do you do when you see something unjust? Are your actions consistent with what you believe?

Lesson 4

Perf...ions
Ex...
...ge Washington,
Politics

Thematic Strands and Primary Questions	Performance Expectations	Student Questions
I. Culture How do belief sys...s, such as religi... political ideals, in...nce culture?	Identify the values and virtues of George Washington, and describe ways his beliefs and attitudes helped shape our country.	What attributes set George Washington apart from other leaders during the crucial founding years of the nation and led others to honor him as a national hero?
X. Civic Ideals and Practices How has the meaning of citizenship evolved, and what is the balance between rights and responsibilities?	Identify and explain the role George Washington played in influencing and shaping public policy and decision making.	What is meant by Washington's distinguished title "father of his country"?
VI. Power, Authority, and Governance How are governments created, structured, and changed?	Analyze and explain ideas and governmental mechanisms to meet needs and wants of citizens, manage conflict, and establish order and security.	What lasting contributions did George Washington make to the United States?
IV. Individual Development and Identity Why do people behave as they do, and how do individuals develop from youth to adulthood?	Relate personal changes to social, cultural, and historical contexts.	How did George Washington's response to British general Braddock's authority compare to his response to the British ten years later?
II. Time, Continuity, and Change What happened in the past, and how am I connected to those in the past?	Use knowledge of facts and concepts drawn from history to inform decision making about taking action on issues.	What new ideas do you have about obeying and resisting authority?

Lesson 5

Thematic Strands and Primary Questions	Performance Expectations	Student Questions
	Benjamin Banneker, Science	
I. Culture How do belief systems, such as religion or political ideals, influence culture?	Explain how experiences may be interpreted by people from diverse cultural perspectives.	What beliefs shaped Benjamin Banneker?
II. Time, Continuity, and Change What happened in the past, and how am I connected to those in the past?	Develop critical sensitivities such as empathy regarding attitudes, values, and behaviors of people in different historical contexts.	What lessons can you learn from the life of Benjamin Banneker?
III. People, Places, and Environments What implications do environmental changes have for people?	Describe physical system changes such as seasons, climate, and weather.	What information about the climate, weather, and seasons can you find in almanacs from the library or on the Internet?
IV. Individual Development and Identity Why do people behave as they do, and how do individuals develop from youth to adulthood?	Describe the ways family, ethnicity, and nationality contribute to personal identity.	What attributes helped Benjamin Banneker achieve his goals? Note the differences and similarities between George Ellicott and Benjamin Banneker.
VIII. Science, Technology, and Society What is the relationship between science and society?	Show through specific examples how science and technology have changed people's perceptions of the world.	How many constellations can you identify on a clear night?
IX. Global Connections How do age-old ethnic enmities impact human rights?	Analyze examples of cooperation and interdependence among groups, societies, and nations.	What are some of the advantages of cross-generational and cross-cultural relationships?

Lesson 6

Thematic Strands and Primary Questions	Performance Expectations	Student Questions
	Haym Salomon, Economics	
IV. Individual Development and Identity Why do people behave as they do?	Evaluate the impact of acts of altruism and other behaviors on individuals and groups.	Why would a Polish immigrant forfeit his own fortune for the Revolutionary War?
VII. Production, Distribution, and Consumption How are goods and services to be distributed?	Explain and illustrate how values and beliefs influence different economic decisions. Apply economic concepts and reasoning when evaluating historical and contemporary social developments and issues.	What beliefs motivated Haym Salomon to make sacrifices for the cause of freedom? What economic and ethical principles can students learn from the life of Haym Salomon? Name two abilities that helped Salomon in his role as "financial hero of the American Revolution."
VI. Power, Authority, and Governance How do nations respond to conflict?	Describe the ways nations and organizations respond to forces of unity and diversity affecting order and security.	List two character traits that marked Salomon's interactions with individuals from other countries, as well as his fellow Patriots. Give an example that illustrates each trait.

Lesson 7

Thematic Strands and Primary Questions	Performance Expectations	Student Questions
	Abigail Adams, Psychology	
I. Culture How do belief systems, such as religion or political ideals, influence culture?	Explain how information and experiences may be interpreted by people from diverse cultural perspectives and frames of reference.	How did Abigail Adams's thirst for knowledge open doors of learning normally closed to women?
II. Time, Continuity, and Change What happened in the past, and how am I connected to those in the past?	Develop critical sensitivities such as empathy and skepticism regarding attitudes, values, and behaviors of people in different historical contexts.	What lessons can both men and women learn from Abigail Adams?
IV. Individual Development and Identity Why do people behave as they do? What influences how people learn, perceive, and grow?	Describe the ways family, religion, gender, and nationality contribute to the development of a sense of self.	What character traits enabled Abigail Adams to become a woman of great influence?
VI. Power, Authority, and Governance How can individual rights be protected within the context of majority rule?	Examine persistent issues involving the rights, roles, and status of the individual in relation to the general welfare.	Describe three ways Abigail Adams advocated for justice and sought to improve the lives of the oppressed. What beliefs do you think formed the foundation for her efforts for social reform?
X. Civic Ideals and Practices What is civic participation, and how can I be involved?	Analyze the effectiveness of selected citizen behaviors in realizing the stated ideals of a democratic republican form of government.	Write a letter of influence to a person in power about an issue in which a person or group is being treated unfairly at home, at school, in the community, or in the world.

Lesson 8

Thematic Strands and Primary Questions	Performance Expectations	Student Questions
	Noah Webster, Law	
IV. Individual Development and Identity Why do people behave as they do?	Relate capabilities, learning, motivation, personality, and behavior to individual development.	What attributes enabled Noah Webster to labor more than twenty years on his dictionary?
I. Culture How do belief systems, such as religion or political ideals, influence culture?	Compare and analyze societal patterns for transmitting culture while adapting to social change.	What core beliefs led to Webster's convictions that the new nation needed an American system of elementary education that promoted patriotism and unity?
II. Time, Continuity, and Change What happened in the past, and how am I connected to those in the past?	Identify and use concepts such as causality and change to show connections among patterns of historical change and continuity.	What lessons can students today learn from an eighteenth-century country teacher?
V. Individuals, Groups, and Institutions What are the roles of institutions in society?	Evaluate the role of institutions in furthering both continuity and change.	List three contributions Noah Webster made to the Patriot cause.
VI. Power, Authority, and Governance How are governments created, structured, and changed?	Describe the purpose of government and how its powers are acquired, used, and justified.	What was the basic difference between the Articles of Confederation and the Constitution?
III. People, Places, and Environments How did settlement patterns affect transmission of culture?	Examine, interpret, and analyze cultural patterns, such as cultural transmission of customs and ideas.	Beyond the educational value of Webster's speller, what deeper significance did the text hold in the early years of the new nation?
X. Civic Ideals and Practices What is the role of a citizen?	Analyze citizen action as it influences public policy.	How did Noah Webster influence public policy?

Lesson 9

Thematic Strands and Primary Questions	Performance Expectations	Student Questions
	John Quincy Adams, Ethics	
IV. Individual Development and Identity Why do people behave as they do?	Identify and describe the influence of attitudes, values, and beliefs on personal identity.	What attributes worked to both the advantage and disadvantage of John Quincy Adams?
I. Culture How do belief systems, such as religion or political ideals, influence culture?	Interpret patterns of behavior reflecting values and attitudes that contribute to cross-cultural understanding.	On what core beliefs did he refuse to compromise in his political and personal decisions?
II. Time, Continuity, and Change What happened in the past, and how am I connected to those in the past?	Investigate, interpret, and analyze multiple historical viewpoints across cultures related to important events while employing empathy, skepticism, and critical judgment.	Compare and contrast the educational experiences of John Quincy Adams to your own.
VIII. Science, Technology, and Society How can we preserve our fundamental values and beliefs in the midst of technological change?	Make judgments about how science and technology have transformed human society and our understanding of time, space, place, and human-environment interactions.	If James Smithson could see the Smithsonian Institution today, what do you think his reaction would be? How successful do you think the Smithsonian has been in fulfilling his hope of increasing knowledge?
IX. Global Connections How do age-old ethnic enmities impact human rights?	Demonstrate understanding of concerns, standards, issues, and conflicts related to universal human rights.	How do you make ethical decisions about what is right and wrong?

Formal Assessments

NCSS Standards

Apply Social Studies Skills—critical thinking skills, differentiating between primary and secondary sources, sequencing, identifying cause-and-effect relationships, finding the main idea, drawing conclusions.

Sequencing

Read the following paragraph and sequence the events in the order they are recorded, from 1 (first) to 5 (last).

In the summer of 1793, a yellow fever epidemic struck Philadelphia. During the next one hundred days, one-tenth of the city's population died. Fear descended on the capital city. Families boarded up their houses and retreated to the country. Panic-stricken citizens crowded roads leading out of Philadelphia, leaving the city streets deserted. Only the creaking wheels of funeral hearses carrying the dead to unmarked graves interrupted the silence. Many physicians fled Philadelphia as the epidemic paralyzed the city. But Dr. Benjamin Rush refused to flee. He also urged his medical apprentices to stay and help the sick. He told them, "I may fall a victim to the epidemic, and so may you, gentlemen. But I prefer, since I am placed here by Divine Providence, to fall in performing my duty." Dr. Rush and his team of students attacked the plague bravely, although their commitment proved treacherous and even deadly.

1. ___ Ten percent of the population of Philadelphia died.

2. ___ Dr. Rush treated the sick patients.

3. ___ A yellow fever epidemic struck Philadelphia.

4. ___ Rush's team of physicians suffered because of their service and commitment.

5. ___ Scared citizens left the streets deserted.

Reading Comprehension and Interpretation

Place on each blank line the letter that best answers the question.

6. ___ Which of the following statements best describes the main idea of the paragraph?

    a. Medical apprentices help the sick.
    b. Yellow fever was a deadly disease in 1793.
    c. Rush and his medical team served the sick of Philadelphia with courage.
    d. Funeral hearses had creaking wheels in the eighteenth century.

7. ___ Which of the following conclusions could not be drawn from the paragraph?

    a. Dr. Rush's example of committed service influenced his students.
    b. Dr. Rush believed God placed him in Philadelphia for a special purpose.
    c. In the eighteenth century, yellow fever was a deadly disease.
    d. Unmarked graves signal a lack of concern for family in Philadelphia.

8. ___ Which of the following cause-and-effect relationships cannot be substantiated from the paragraph?

    a. Medical training leads physicians to serve others with commitment.
    b. Yellow fever was less widespread in the countryside than it was in the city limits.
    c. The yellow fever epidemic caused fear.
    d. Fear of disease left Philadelphia streets deserted.

Identifying Primary and Secondary Sources

Read the following quotations and determine whether they are primary or secondary sources. Place a P for primary or an S for secondary in the corresponding blanks.

9. ___ "The Cold was so extremely severe, that Mr. Gist had all his Fingers, and some of his Toes frozen, and the Water was shut up so hard, that we found no Difficulty in getting off the Island on the Ice in the Morning, and went to Mr. Frazier's." (George Washington, *The Maryland Gazette*, March 21, 1754)

10. ___ "In a single night, 9,000 troops had escaped across the river. Not a life was lost. The only men captured were three who had hung back to plunder." (David McCullough, *1776*, 2005)

11. ___ "At the time of his death in 1813, newspapers, Founding Fathers, and other leaders of the day heralded Benjamin Rush as one of America's three most notable individuals, ranking him with George Washington and Benjamin Franklin." (David Barton, *Benjamin Rush: Signer of the Declaration of Independence*, 1999)

12. ___ "The debate grew heated, threatening to break up the convention, and on June 11 Franklin decided it was time to try to restore a spirit of compromise." (Walter Isaacson, *Benjamin Franklin: An American Life*, 2003)

13. ___ "I think you ladies are in the number of the best patriots America can boast." (George Washington, in a letter to Annis Boudinot Stockton, August 31, 1788)

Identifying Historical Figures

Match each historical figure in the first column with his/her description in the second column by writing the corresponding letter in the blank.

14. ___ William Bradford
15. ___ John Winthrop
16. ___ Benjamin Franklin
17. ___ Benjamin Rush
18. ___ George Washington
19. ___ Haym Salomon
20. ___ Benjamin Banneker
21. ___ Abigail Adams
22. ___ Noah Webster
23. ___ John Quincy Adams

a. wife and mother of U.S. presidents

b. "father of American medicine"

c. Revolutionary War financier

d. author of textbooks and dictionaries

e. "father of his country"

f. Pilgrim governor of the Plymouth colony

g. Puritan leader of Massachusetts Bay Colony

h. surveyor of Washington DC

i. advocate for Smithsonian Institution

j. printer, inventor, and statesman

Recalling Historical Facts

Write a T for true or an F for false in the blank before each of the following statements.

24. ___ The Puritans of the Massachusetts Bay Colony extended religious freedom to all the colonists settling in Massachusetts.

25. ___ In the Mayflower Compact, the Pilgrims listed spreading the Christian faith as one of four reasons they came to America.

26. ___ Many of the signers of the Declaration of Independence suffered great losses as a result of their efforts for the new nation.

27. ___ The diplomatic skills of Dr. Benjamin Franklin were invaluable in securing the help of the French during the Revolutionary War.

28. ___ When British general Howe trapped General George Washington and his troops on Long Island, Washington preserved his army with a harrowing nighttime escape across the East River.

29. ___ Benjamin Franklin was unanimously elected as president of the Constitutional Convention.

30. ___ John Quincy Adams mediated the reconciliation between his father, John Adams, and Thomas Jefferson.

31. ___ John Adams and Thomas Jefferson died on the same day (July 4, 1826)— exactly fifty years after they had both signed the Declaration of Independence.

32. ___ The United States treasury repaid Haym Salomon the money he loaned the government during the Revolutionary War.

33. ___ Haym Salomon escaped notorious British prisons twice by using his financial assets and his language abilities.

34. ___ When he was nearly sixty years old, Benjamin Rush learned astronomy and surveying, and he was selected to survey the land for the new Federal District (now Washington DC).

35. ___ Since Benjamin Banneker wanted to be recognized only because of his scientific achievements, he refused to be involved in the antislavery cause.

36. ___ Although Abigail Adams came from a prominent New England family, she received almost no formal education.

37. ___ Abigail Adams served as a spy during the Revolutionary War.

38. ___ In completing his masterpiece—his comprehensive dictionary—Noah Webster worked more than twenty years and learned more than twenty languages.

39. ___ John Quincy Adams's immense popularity as a two-term president led to his election to the U.S. House of Representatives, where he served seventeen years.

Recognizing Government Documents

Match each historical document in the first column with the correct description by writing the corresponding letter on the blank.

40. ___ Mayflower Compact

41. ___ Declaration of Independence

42. ___ Articles of Confederation

43. ___ U.S. Constitution

44. ___ Bill of Rights

a. announced America's freedom from England

b. governmental document establishing system of checks and balances

c. Pilgrim document that established self-government based on the idea of "the consent of the governed"

d. first ten amendments to U.S. Constitution

e. established a weak central government for the thirteen colonies of the United States of America

Identifying Civic Virtues

Match each character trait in the first column with a historical event in the second column that reflects the civic virtue. (Some events demonstrate more than one virtue.)

45. ___ self-control

46. ___ humor

47. ___ perseverance

48. ___ courage

49. ___ influence

50. ___ patience

51. ___ generosity

52. ___ determination

53. ___ peacemaking

54. ___ faith

a. Dr. Rush helped resolve a bitter dispute between his friends Thomas Jefferson and John Adams.

b. Knowing when to wait and when to act, General George Washington ferried his troops across the river at night in escape, but later launched a surprise attack, winning a decisive victory at the Battle of Trenton.

c. Haym Salomon sacrificially loaned his personal funds to individual Patriots, as well as to the struggling government in support of the cause of freedom.

d. Noah Webster worked over two decades defining 70,000 words for his dictionary.

e. "Yes, we must, indeed, all hang together—or most assuredly we shall all hang separately!" said Benjamin Franklin after signing the Declaration of Independence.

f. As her husband worked on the Declaration of Independence, Abigail Adams seized the opportunity to rally in support of women by writing, "Remember the ladies."

g. Sacrificing comfort and safety, the Pilgrims traveled to America in search of religious freedom.

h. Using borrowed instruments, Benjamin Banneker carefully calculated every figure for his almanac and tried repeatedly to find a publisher.

i. Though arrows and bullets flew all around and tore into his uniform, George Washington rode to all parts of the battlefield carrying out the general's orders.

j. John Quincy Adams doggedly guarded the Smithson fortune, insisting that it be used for its intended purposes.

Vocabulary

Match each word in the first column with its corresponding definition in the second column.

55. ___ espionage

56. ___ abolition

57. ___ almanac

58. ___ Providence

59. ___ apprentice

60. ___ phonetics

61. ___ securities

62. ___ pilgrim

63. ___ etymology

64. ___ boycott

65. ___ Dissenters

66. ___ eloquent

67. ___ waver

68. ___ eulogy

69. ___ maxim

70. ___ secular

71. ___ wampum

72. ___ Deist

73. ___ reformer

74. ___ solitude

75. ___ reconcile

a. group that disagreed with or objected to the established religious authority

b. a temporary resident on earth who is traveling through life on a journey to heaven

c. one bound by a legal agreement to serve for a period of time to learn a trade or art

d. speech given in honor of a deceased person

e. a saying or short piece of wisdom

f. pertaining to the world; distinguished from the spiritual

g. beads used by Native Americans as money

h. to sway back and forth between opinions

i. one who believes God created the world but now exercises no direct control over it

j. one who seeks to change or improve conditions

k. to bring harmony; settle differences

l. the act of spying on others to obtain information about a foreign government

m. the withholding of business to make a statement or bring about change

n. the history of a word

o. the study of speech sounds in a language

p. capable and expressive in the use of words

q. investment documents, such as stock certificates or bonds

r. a state of being alone and quiet

s. book or chart containing a calendar based on astronomy

t. the act of doing away with, especially relating to slavery

u. God

Essay

Choose one of the following prompts and write an essay in response. Explain your answer using two historical and two modern examples. (25 points)

1. How did the Founders understand the relationship between church and state, and in what ways has this relationship changed?

2. How can a religiously diverse nation balance respect for all backgrounds with its moral foundation?

3. Do you think a free society can succeed without people of faith?

Formal Assessment Answer Keys

Sequencing
1. 2
2. 4
3. 1
4. 5
5. 3

**Reading
Comprehension
and Interpretation**
6. c
7. d
8. a

**Identifying
Primary and
Secondary Sources**
9. P
10. S
11. S
12. S
13. P

**Identifying
Historical Figures**
14. f
15. g
16. j
17. b
18. e
19. c
20. h
21. a
22. d
23. i

**Recalling
Historical Facts**
24. F
25. T
26. T
27. T
28. T
29. F
30. F
31. T
32. F
33. T
34. F
35. F
36. T
37. T
38. T
39. F

**Recognizing
Government
Documents**
40. c
41. a
42. e
43. b
44. d

**Identifying
Civic Virtues**
45. b
46. e
47. d, h, j
48. e, g, i
49. a, f
50. b, h
51. c
52. g, j
53. a
54. g

Vocabulary
55. l
56. t
57. s
58. u
59. c
60. o
61. q
62. b
63. n
64. m
65. a
66. p
67. h
68. d
69. e
70. f
71. g
72. i
73. j
74. r
75. k